The Psychology of Schizophrenia

A Selection of Classic Articles on the Analysis and Symptoms of Schizophrenia

By

Various Authors

British Library Cataloguing-in-Publication Data
A catalogue record for this book is available from
the British Library

Contents

SCHIZOPHRENIA

There is one word of advice for the beginner who contemplates analysing a case of established or incipient schizophrenia—literally one word—it is: "Don't!"

On the other hand it was held by Bleuler, who first coined this term in 1911, that all functional mental disturbances, with the exception of manic-depressive psychosis, all psychogenic disorders, including all abnormalities of mental make-up, were manifestations of schizophrenia. Bleuler had thus extended and increased the scope of Kraepelin's (1896) description of dementia praecox. Schizophrenia he described as a morbid process characterised by the "splitting of the mind", resulting in an increasing withdrawal of interest from the environment (introversion) together with "a disorder of feeling, of conduct and of thought".

If there is any truth in Bleuler's view, probably every case, or almost every case, which we analyse has at least a modicum of this morbid process at work within it. Therefore, although it is impracticable to analyse established schizophrenia outside an institution, it is advisable for the would-be analyst to try to understand the essentials of its psychopathology, if only because of the possibility that it has ramifications within the interstices of almost every mind which he will analyse.

Attempts to attribute it primarily to bodily changes, such as those of endocrine disorder (Kraepelin, Bleuler, Mott, Alzheimer and others) or those of faulty metabolism (Gjessing, Lorenz, Levenhart and others), though undertaken with great care and perseverance by a succession of competent observers, have led to a surprising absence of any concrete conclusions. For instance, Dunlap, after particularly careful investigation with schizophrenic cases and control cases, came to the conclusion that previous observers, including Alzheimer, were mistaken and that "schizophrenia is a condition lacking in any fundamental or constant alteration in nerve cells".

The fact, though a negative one, that no concrete conclusions in regard to organic or physiological changes can be maintained in our present state of knowledge, is of the utmost importance as evidence that the trouble is primarily psychological, and as evidence of the extraordinarily far-reaching effects that can finally result from psychological processes—if indeed evidence were needed.

Adolf Meyer, one of the chief exponents of the psychological point of view, regards schizophrenia "as the outcome of progressive maladaptation of the individual to his environment". In his view it is an extreme manifestation of a probable "reaction type"—"the end-result of an accumulation of faulty habits of reaction".

When we consider in conjunction with this view that approximately half the cases have a family record of mental illness, the aetiological position as between hereditary causes and acquired reactions becomes somewhat complicated unless we revert to a discredited Lamarckian hypothesis that acquired characters may be inherited, in which case we have only to consider this reaction-hypothesis of Meyer's as extending through a succession of generations, to be able to credit it finally with the production of schizophrenia.

It is not possible in the present chapter to go into all the problems of the Lamarckian as against the Weismann theory (of the continuation of the germ plasm alone), but I may mention in passing that this is only one of innumerable considerations which, in spite of the biologists, leads me to regard a total exclusion of Lamarckism as short-sighted. The operation of Lamarckism in some form or another is the only possibility of accounting for not only the production of such disorders as schizophrenia together with all other deep-seated psychogenic disorders, but of also accounting for the essential evolutionary principle of biological adaptation to environment.

In short, Lamarckism pits the evidence of the whole biosphere against the isolated instances of the experimental biologist.

From the evidences of family history it would seem that schizophrenia is a disorder the roots of which lie deeper than the individual, probably affect the germ plasm and are transmittable. In this connection it is interesting to note that many of the physical investigators found, or thought they found, a disordered secretion of the sex glands. My view would be that functionally a disorder of the mind cannot leave unaffected the function of sexuality, nor vice versa. This is not unrelated to heredity, transmittability and Lamarckism in general. It may be possible to return to a consideration of the psychopathology of this illness after we shall have studied a few examples.

In spite of the formal divisions of the illness into three or four main groups, for instance according to Kraepelin (1) the "Simplex", (2) the "Hebephrenic", (3) the "Katatonic" and (4) the "Paranoid", the impression of the psychotherapist who comes into contact with the borderline rather than with established cases is that there are as many varieties as there are individuals. No two cases are the same, though large numbers of patients may show some element of a morbid process characteristic of or analogous to schizophrenia. Indeed, it might be said that the conception of "mental conflict", the primary factor in all psychogenic symptom-production, is in some degree synonymous with Bleuler's "splitting of the mind". Indeed, apart from debilitating illness such as influenza, it is commonly some current conflict, such as a love affair, worry over masturbation or a sexual incident, which precipitates the breakdown, though it is afterwards discovered that a movement towards it had been going on insidiously long before. The symptomatology varies greatly according to the severity of the particular stage of the illness, but a constant characteristic is some degree of detachment from reality either emotional or intellectual or both. The patient may show natural apathy and indifference with perhaps mild depression and a feeling of failure, or he may be dreamy and full of ruminations with a failure to respond adequately to events around, which should ordinarily cause some affective response. Often a queer disharmony between the patient's thought and his mood can be detected. He may smile while thinking or speaking of something distressing, or less commonly, his eyes fill with tears at something ordinarily cheerful. This is because his emotional response is in accordance with his phantasy life, irrespective of the current distraction of comparatively superficial realities.

At a later stage of the illness there will of course be even more marked changes in his personality, and these may be shown by slovenly behaviour and disregard for his appearance. Sooner or later in a case which is well on the way to established schizophrenia there will be ideas of reference, as, for instance, that people are making actions mocking him, illusions and hallucinations, particularly of hearing voices (*e.g.* commenting upon his secret thoughts), and delusions, sometimes of his outstanding importance. However, his delusions are not systematised as they are in paranoia. In contrast to these grave symptoms, there is relatively no disorientation of space or time, or impairment of memory or intellectual faculties as such, although he is so seriously out of touch with reality.

It has been said that all mental disorders represent stages in a one-and-only mental disorder, namely, disintegration of the mind, or dementia. Observation of advanced cases of schizophrenia seems to support this conception as so large a proportion of them become steadily worse until they are truly demented, and unless mute, display complete incoherence, with the familiar so-called "word-salad".

(1) According to Kraepelin's varieties the schizophrenia "Simplex" comes about insidiously. For instance, a mother has been known to say that her daughter "has not really altered; she has only gradually grown more and more like herself". The general impression of detachment from reality, either emotional or intellectual or both, is accompanied by a lack of ambition and either a general contentment with an idle, unprogressive life, or a hopeless and impractical dissatisfaction.

(2) The "Hebephrenic" variety is also difficult to differentiate, seeming to lie between the "Simplex" and the "Katatonic" types. There is usually, though not always, a history of tantrums or neurotic tendencies, and the introverted individual seems to become more completely introverted, not bothering to go out or perhaps even to rise from the chair. If, however, you can get him to talk, you may be surprised at the amount of emotion that lies under his shut-in exterior. There is often not only emotional disturbance, but considerable incoherence. Hallucinations of hearing and sometimes of sight are particularly common in this variety. There are also abundant ideas of reference and probably a history of a good deal of senseless conduct.

(3) The characteristic of the "Katatonic" variety is an alternation between what is called "catatonic stupor", a usually more pronounced retreat even than that of the "Hebephrenic", and outbursts of an extraordinary excitement. In the dull, stuporous stage the patient will be mute, often with a refusal of food, a vacant expression, and stand like a mummy taking no interest in anything. There are a large number of mannerisms, and in

advanced cases extraordinary symptoms and signs, including signs of bad circulation of the extremities shown by a blueness of the arms and a phenomenon called *flexibilitas cerea*, which means that whatever odd attitude a limb is placed in he will retain it in that position for a considerable time. There may also be such symptoms as echolalia and echopraxia, which mean respectively a parrot-like repetition of what one says to him instead of answering one's question, and a senseless imitation of one's gestures. From this shut-in position the patient may burst into a violent frenzy without any warning and perform any violent act to himself or others. He is not intentionally homicidal but acts impulsively, probably in response to some hallucinations.

(4) The "Paranoid" varieties usually come on considerably later in life. Physical changes are not so marked, though there may be a number of complaints of a physical nature. One of the main features of this variety is delusions, not so systematised as those of paranoia proper. Nevertheless many modern authors have separated this group from schizophrenia and included it under the possibly related reaction-type group of "Paranoia, Paraphrenia and Paranoid Types".

However valuable these classifications are to the psychiatrist practising in mental hospitals, they are not so useful to the psychotherapist who has to deal not with the clear or established cases, but with very minor forms of an analogous if not identical "mind-splitting" process. Farrar's idea of five main types of shut-in personality is more useful to psychotherapy than the orthodox psychiatric divisions into three or four groups characteristic of advanced cases. Farrar distinguishes (1) the Backward Type; (2) the Precocious, Studious Type; (3) the Neurotic Type; (4) the Asocial, Seclusive Type; and (5) the Juvenile Type. The psychotherapist is all too familiar with the difficulties presented by each one of these various introverted types, if indeed he does not in some cases completely miss the essential relationship of his patient to this disease. To illustrate this I will first give a few brief instances of patients who have been sent to me for treatment and then a longer case history of a patient who though not schizophrenic in the asylum sense can be classified only under that category.

The first case is one which belongs quite clearly to Farrar's "Juvenile Type". She is a woman in the early thirties who looks so young that she is frequently being humiliated by being taken for a child. For instance, going with a party to a licensed hotel she was refused admission by the proprietor, who would not be moved! She was sent to me because she was getting very depressed and weeping in her home atmosphere, complaining of a general lack of interest in things, was nervy and irritable with a show of tantrums.

When she saw me she had very little to complain of except that she had lost confidence in herself (though it transpired that she never had had any confidence), that she did not seem to do anything right and was usually rather depressed.

She said: "I seem to be very little use, and there does not seem to be much object in my living at all."

She later admitted that there was nothing new about this, as ever since the age of fourteen she had always wondered why people were born or why they went on living. She found life far too much to cope with and particularly avoided all social contact, and indeed contact even with relatives or friends. Her slow method of thinking and speaking gave the impression of stupidity, and one might have confused such a case with a high-grade mental defective, but the fact was that this young woman had had a high standard of scholastic education and was indeed a university graduate!

My justification for placing her tentatively under the heading of borderline schizophrenia of Farrar's Juvenile Type is partly because her emotional life was confined to day-dreaming and that she had, in all emotional relationships at least as well as in many other ways, retreated from almost all reality contacts. Even this dream life she had not made fully conscious and certainly had never mentioned it to anybody. It was some time before it emerged. It proved to be an extraordinary saga of the romantic-novel type of adventure. But even there she herself was not one of the characters in the romance, although it was noticeable that the heroine bore her name! The chief adventures of this heroine were those of romantic marriage and reproduction. Hero and heroine became the parents of a family, the family grew, and one of the daughters, in turn with a name like her own, would marry and in turn reproduce, and so on with much detail throughout many generations. This dream life was her sole form of recreation.

These dreams contrasted markedly with her reality behaviour, for emotionally, bodily and in time and space she always closed up and backed away hurriedly from any and every eligible male contact. Indeed, she was totally unaware of any sexual inclination throughout her life. Nevertheless the relating of her dream sagas, which had been going on unspoken for over a decade, apparently set things moving within her, for she duly became conscious of what appeared to be normal desires for love and sex. At the same time some improvement took place in her social life and sociability. Though she has since gone abroad in the hope of marrying—a hope backed by some real libidinal desire—and although she indulges in erotic phantasies, some of which are accompanied by complete sexual orgasm, my knowledge of her psychopathology makes me of the opinion that she would in sexual congress suffer from frigidity, and that further improvement would be difficult to achieve. Persons who have failed to grow up by the time they are well over twenty may well be the despair of the analyst.

Her psychopathology may throw a little light upon that far more advanced condition called Schizophrenia Simplex. The lack of ambition from which these patients suffer was common to this girl also before she came for treatment, and analysis revealed quite clearly that this lack of ambition was due to *lack of libidinal drive*. It revealed also that the reason for this lack of libidinal drive was because her libido, instead of overcoming the inhibiting effects of parents and family, had either remained inhibited or had regressed to a childish or infantile level. Her emotional age, which was still that of about thirteen or earlier, represented a stage when, with the onset of the menses, she had violently repressed all sexual thoughts and feelings from reaching consciousness or achieving any further degree of maturity.

At one stage in her analysis, when she was for the first time becoming conscious of sexual feelings, she dreamt that she was running away in a car from a riotous mob which would have seized and destroyed her. In association of thought she said: "If I had not come for analysis the sexual feelings would have been held in check, and then there wouldn't have been all this rioting business. When I first came here I had some idea that you'd help me to *get rid* of my day-dreams because I *couldn't control* them any more and they were getting more and more hold over me and overpowering me more and more, so that I seemed to have lost all interest in everything else in life."

This may cause us to reflect as to whether "Introversion" is really synonymous with unconscious sexual phantasy, and as to whether this is the essence of the initial movement in schizophrenia.

Later this patient said: "In getting away from the riotous mob I was trying to get back to mother and father. I have felt that I should never have left them for a moment. That's why I wanted to get rid of the day-dreams too. I felt like a child who had walked out of a nice comfortable home to see what the night was like and couldn't find its way back. I used to depend on mother and father for a comfortable background, and I suppose for comfortable *feelings*. The day-dreams were a compromise—half and half—but the riotous mob was terrifying. Instead of getting rid of my day-dreams this treatment has brought up something worse."

Evidently her case is an extreme example of the familiar conflict between developing sexuality and the primitive and repressing fixation to parent imagos. As she says, the day-dreams were the introverted compromise between the two sides of the conflict, absorbing almost all her libidinal energy and her life. The resistance to mature sexual development and extraversion is evident.

It may be suggested that in this case some hypo-function of the pituitary could account for both her childish appearance and emotional anaemia. Though I would not deny such a possibility, I still think it is unjustifiable to assume that such hypo-function must be primary (perhaps magical) and (if present) that it cannot itself be secondary to emotional retardation psychologically initiated.

Analysing such patients, whether or not they may be regarded as on the outer fringes of schizophrenia, may well throw some light upon the nature of schizophrenic mechanisms which it is often impossible to trace in more advanced cases of the illness. When we get to a slightly more schizophrenic case than the one just described we are apt to meet with technical difficulties during analysis.

For instance, I have had patients who, lying on the analytical settee, and showing the usual vague ideas and affects of the schizophrenic, suddenly developed disorders of conduct—while one was still trying to see rhyme or reason in their rather intangible but interesting mutterings. One such patient, for example, would refuse to leave the consulting-room at the end of his analytical hour, it commonly taking ten minutes or more to persuade him to make way for the next case. If he did rise from the settee he would then stand in a catatonic attitude in the middle of the floor, silent and impervious to words or attempts to lead him out. Any attempt to draw him by the hand or to push him gently or firmly resulted in a stolid mule-like resistance (Negativism). I soon overcame this difficulty by making him the last patient of the day and leaving him alone in the room to find his own way out, but in due course he learned to anticipate my departure, and I would find him holding the handle of the door of my car, necessitating similar delays and persuasions on the pavement outside. He admitted during the sessions that he was again a baby clinging to a much-needed mother, but the splitting of his mind was such that these and several more extraordinary samples of insight made little or no difference to his actual conduct. Though analysis had to be stopped on account of such difficulties, I may say that for over ten years this patient has avoided the need for mental hospital treatment. Nevertheless, the reason I would advise against treating any established schizophrenic case is that however quiescent, "Simplex" or "Hebephrenic" they may appear to be, there is, until we know our patient very well indeed, the danger of an outburst of catatonic frenzy—for which the analyst may be unfairly blamed.

Against this I will give a short example of a fairly typical hebephrenic in whose case I found it helpful to establish a transference in order to gratify her parents' wishes that she should be persuaded to have convulsive therapy without having to be certified or enter a mental hospital. The following are her remarks at the first interview recorded verbatim.

She says: "The chief trouble is that for a long time now everything I do or think seems to cause some commotion and there is always a lot of talk about it. If a memory comes to me, it seems to bring some voices making a remark about it or repeating it. Sometimes it seems to be shouted about the place."

ANALYST: "*How long has this been going on?*"

PATIENT: "Over two years. It began with influenza and a general breakdown which I had. It has been up and down ever since. I have had it brought to my mind by voices or whispers. If I get a pain it is remarked about by voices. Some are men's voices and some women's voices and some the voices of children.

It is so difficult to express. It is so real and disturbing and tormenting. Very often mad things come to your brain and you do not want to be tormented by them afterwards."

ANALYST: "*What mad things for instance?*"

PATIENT: "It is mad to think that the next-door neighbours are listening-in to my brain."

ANALYST: "*Do you mean that they are really listening-in directly to what your brain is doing?*"

PATIENT: "I don't know. I cannot help feeling it because of the repetition I hear and the discussion afterwards. I have tried hard to think it is just imagination, but I cannot. It seems someone's got a *plan* of my brain and as different parts of me work so they know."

ANALYST: "*For example?*"

PATIENT: "If I scratch my neck I hear it repeated, 'She's scratching her neck.' The last few days I have had an irritation of my back passage and when I have been in bed scratching it I have heard remarks about it. Sometimes the voices are my neighbours, sometimes other people I have met."

ANALYST: "*Do you think it could be a part of your own mind doing this?*"

PATIENT: "No. I don't think so. I don't think it is my own mind. It is different voices and some of the voices I do not recognise. It makes you feel so hopeless. It has been the same for eighteen months and it is most embarrassing sometimes. For instance at my period every time I put on another towel there has been talk about it, even shouting about it. I have tried to get hardened to it, but I feel it should not be. Sometimes I let off some curses." (She has been known to run out of the house and reprimand the neighbours volubly from the street—a performance which, of course, everybody failed to understand.)

She continued: "It is irritating to feel that people somewhere know what you are doing. Also in bed I get a feeling of pressure as though people are over me doing things to my body. It is horrible to think that they can give me pain in my eyes or head and that I can keep nothing to myself that is private. It is like a wireless set in my head that anybody can pick up. Sometimes I have heard three different voices; one telling me not to do a thing, the second telling me to do it, and a third, which is my own voice, steering in between the other two."

This is clearly a case of schizophrenia of the hebephrenic type.

Her history shows that she has hitherto had no outbursts of catatonic excitement except perhaps of the very minor degree of her rather emotional outbursts reprimanding her "tormentors". I may add that after a few sessions this patient, contrary to what many suppose happens in these "narcissistic" illnesses, showed signs of a considerable degree of transference and was completely obedient to my advice, attending for some eighteen bi-weekly electric convulsive therapy treatments. Fortunately she was one of those who showed an appreciable degree of improvement. The voices grew fainter and more distant with almost every shock. What was left of them she easily learned to ignore and was able to take up some part-time work. But they never completely disappeared. It took a bomb explosion which buried her under the debris of her house, from which she was dug almost suffocated some six hours later, to effect the final and apparently complete cure. Every vestige of her hallucinations vanished from the moment of recovery from that last experience. However, in a case as pronounced as this, one would be wiser to regard the apparent cure in the nature of a remission brought about by shock and not to be surprised if the illness recurs even after many years of relative normality.

Looking for a patient who may throw more light upon the psychopathology of the schizophrenic process and be able to correlate our findings with those of the psychopathology of neuroses in general, I think of a man in the middle forties who, though not so typical a schizophrenic as the previous case, is undoubtedly very introverted and narcissistic and whose conduct has been such that he could hardly be placed under any other classification than that of a borderline schizophrenic. He is now approaching middle-age and is, or rather was, a university lecturer, which gives some idea of his intellectual attainment. His interests are very academic and he is liable to waste endless days and weeks discussing learned metaphysical obscurities instead of the relevant material for which he has come for analysis. He is scholarly, well-bred and with a gentle and emotionally neutral disposition. He has become particularly interested in a succession of cults, such as occultism, and has periods during which he starves himself for idealistic reasons. He is impervious to emotional disturbances around him to the extent even of appearing emotionally detached.

With all this gentleness, so common in the schizophrenic

reaction type, his history includes behaviour which characterises schizophrenia or the schizoid character. For instance, though moderately wealthy, he has spent months as a disreputable tramp leading a nomadic life and sleeping in gorse bushes and open fields, winter and summer, getting soaked to the skin and letting his clothes dry on him, going without food and getting frequently taken up by the police as a suspicious character. Twice he has been placed in a mental hospital, diagnosed as schizophrenia, and certified. He has indulged in other behaviour totally incongruous with his intellectual attainments and social position. He has gone in for stunts such as scaling scaffolding on buildings to great heights, walking through rivers up to his face in water, jumping on and off trains, running round and round a London square until he dropped and was picked up by the inevitable policeman; and once he tried to board a bus in Piccadilly by levitation. He broke his collar-bone and got himself into hospital. But he did not complain of these things. He complains of what he calls a "lack of spontaneity" and a "lack of feeling". He says he is quite incapable of spontaneity and of emotion, and some of his behaviour at least was evidently with a view to "*forcing himself to be spontaneous and to feel some emotion!*"

At his first interview he told me that he felt the absence of any guide from within to tell him how to act as other people acted, particularly in regard to the opposite sex, but this lack of spontaneity included any and every form of behaviour. In its absence he had no other course but to direct his behaviour with his ego as there were apparently no instinct urges to prompt him. He said the only way he could live was to go through the motions of living, copying those which other people appeared to do. It was not very satisfactory as it was a continuous effort, brought no reward, and somehow or other he always made a mess of it.

It was not easy at first to get him to give particular instances. When asked for an example he would say:

"My trouble is as soon as I put one foot on the accelerator I jam the other on the brake. In any case I have no feeling in the matter. I do not even feel real in myself. I simply must do something about it."

It later appeared that what he had been "doing about it" was trying to accost young women whom he saw in public places. Apparently his object was not that he wanted to get to know them or necessarily to have any relationship with them, but simply that he felt it his duty to himself to force himself into this form of activity principally because he had no real inclination for it! When I insisted that presumably there was an inclination of some sort, he finally admitted that his only inclination would be to retreat and to retire into solitude, but manifestly that was no good, that is what he had done all his life and it had got him nowhere and never would. He used a metaphor which cannot fail to be symbolically interesting to the analyst. He said:

"My Jack has been shut up in its box. All my life it has been shut up. That means that I have not lived at all, not yet. I have never felt any real emotion. I simply *must* let it out or *make* it come out or I might as well be dead now."

Apparently this accounts for, though does not fully explain, some of his stunt behaviour. When asked when his Jack became so completely and permanently shut up he immediately referred to an incident at the age of five years. He said:

"A little boy and girl were brought to play with my sister and me. I took an aversion to the boy, but I fell for the girl. I therefore left the boy with my sister. I was having a glorious time with the little girl and I was so engrossed in playing with her that I did not understand my sister's shrieks and yells. Either I did not understand or I chose to take no notice. The little boy had been ill-treating my sister. My mother arrived on the scene and went for me about it. She said I was the oldest and she expected me to look after the others and I had betrayed her trust."

As is usual in analysis the first reference to a traumatic incident proves to be very incomplete. Later this same incident was again referred to and elaborated.

He explained that until the birth of the other child he had been the apple of his mother's eye. Everything he did was wonderful and he luxuriated in his omnipotent position. With the arrival of his sister, when he was barely three years of age, the whole universe changed. He was completely displaced, and now, instead of being the spoilt and petted baby, he was expected to be the little man or rather the "governess", willingly and gratefully yielding everything in favour of the beloved new arrival.

The incident to which he referred was one which had brought nis altered position home to him in a particularly traumatic manner. He said later:

"My scare was due to mother's anger which I could not understand. All I can remember is that I was absolutely aghast. *My wits left me.* I was knocked clean out. It was a sort of 'death' from which I have never recovered. I think from that incident I shut off my personality, or feelings, as independent of my mother's direction and influence. Mother picked me up by the scruff of the neck and shouted: 'You naughty boy. You dare to leave your sister to be ill-treated and selfishly amuse yourself with a little girl!'

"I was absolutely flabbergasted. I was so happy playing with the little girl. In fact I think I was so happy that that is why I did not notice my sister's screams. Then suddenly I saw my mother approaching like a hurricane, or like an avenging Nemesis. She would not speak until she got hold of me. I think as I saw her my mind went for any possible wrong I might have done and I did not find anything, and therefore I was quite unprepared for the onslaught. Since then I have never stuck up for myself. I have been completely submerged. Her anger was to me like the vengeance of God with a justness in it because it came from her and she could not be guilty of wrong. I was sort of hypnotised by the descending vengeance and I have been hypnotised ever since. I have never really thought I have had a leg to stand on. I could only conclude that anything I did on my own account, for pleasure, was utterly wrong. In fact the idea would terrify me. There was only one course for me to pursue from that moment, and that was to repress completely any inclination or feeling I had . . . any desires. And as repressing these *and* being aware of them is a painful experience, *it is better not to be aware of them at all.* That is why I feel nothing. I would not be allowed to express it or take pleasure in it if I did feel it, so it is better not even to feel it."

Later he says: "If I wanted to make mother take notice of me and made advances to her and clung around her skirt, she would always repulse me, tell me I was the elder child and I had to try to be a man, or else freeze me up, or blitz me. In some such way I learnt that my instincts were absolutely wrong, especially if I was inclined in any way to be cocky. But now I have seen quite clearly that I was wrong in denying my instincts and looking at them as the original sin that had to be trampled upon. That is why I have been trying to do things ever since *as though* I had the instinct urge behind them."

At the next session the patient refused to lie down! Instead he insisted upon sitting up and facing me. It was a demonstration of the return of his "cockiness", this time directed against me in lieu of mother. He said: "What I want to talk about, what concerns me, is this difficulty in contacting women."

I said: "Instead of calling them 'women' shall we call them 'mother', it may make it clearer." But on this occasion he ignored my remark and went on to describe his "unwarranted" hesitations in speaking to young women whom he saw in public places and felt he should use for the purpose of exercising his utterly repressed self-assertion.

Very soon we arrived at a session which spelt crisis. There may have been an hysterical element in it, but my general impression was that it differed from the usual analytical crisis of the hysteric in that he had not even a dim consciousness of play-acting. He arrived late, stood at the front door and said it was no good his staying. He had merely come through his wretched "super-ego" telling him he might as well be polite to me and tell me in person that he was not coming. I told him of course that it was quite right to tell me all this, but it should be told while he lay on the settee. He stood with his hand on the handle of the front door and it took ten minutes to persuade him to enter the consulting-room. He proceeded to throw himself about on the analytical settee in great concern at the way he had typically and wretchedly messed-up an opportunity to let out his self-assertion in relation to a woman.

He said: "I was feeling a little self-assertion and then my blessed super-ego came along and said 'Your Jack has come too far out of the box. Now push it back again.' "

It was not easy to get him to tell the story consecutively, but he made some attempt.

"I felt panic all yesterday afternoon and I could not talk to the girl because I felt whatever I did would be wrong. I suppose it was because I felt a bit self-assertive."

ANALYST: "*You have not told me the circumstances. You are keeping me in the dark.*"

PATIENT: "I got a bit of an erection."

ANALYST: "*Well, what were the circumstances? Were you with the lady?*"

He said: "No, we were not anywhere near each other, in fact she was in another town (!) It was not any question of being together or anything like that; only she was with me in thought. It was that particular girl I told you about once before."

ANALYST: "*Well, seeing that she was not even there, how do we know it was her for whom you got these feelings?*"

He said: "Who was it then?"

ANALYST: "*I can tell you who it was.*"

PATIENT: "Who?"

ANALYST: "*Your mother.*"

PATIENT (ignoring my remark): "Then the panic came."

ANALYST: "*Naturally! If you get an erection for your mother, of course you panic.*"

PATIENT: "Then I had no feelings at all."

ANALYST: "*You were trying to stop the terrible consequences of the phantasy with your mother.*"

PATIENT: "I can quite agree with it. I have had little insights like that before, but to me it is only a label."

ANALYST: "*A label that reduces you to panic.*"

PATIENT: "My ego can only stand up and watch, so numbed that it cannot even *think* leave alone *feel*. I presume that that is associated with a memory of displaying affectionate emotion to my mother and being met by cold anger as used to be the case . . . as though she were acting for the Almighty, meting out punishment . . . it is more than anger . . . it is more righteous indignation . . . and there is some memory that sometime or other I must have run to her happy . . . I wanted to throw my arms round her . . . and I was met and flabbergasted by angry chastisement."

ANALYST: "*And it is still going on.*"

(A point of analytical interest is that this interpretation of "mother" for the girl has brought his mind to recount these remembrances of infancy.)

PATIENT: "The only thing my super-ego can do is to provoke me. Every time I let my Jack creep out of the box it is met by a fierce, angry storm. Do you wonder that I was flabbergasted, scared out of my wits? How did I know what was going to happen? I was full of affection and she simply turned on me.

"So I imagine any girl I meet is going to turn on me and rend me. She is going to catch me off my guard."

He then goes on to relate an incident earlier than the one at five. He says: "I wanted to restore the situation with my mother that had existed before the sister was born where I would be the one she loved. I saw that baby that had taken my place, lying in a pram. Perhaps I was only three or four, but I saw my opportunity. I pushed that pram to where it would run away by itself down the hill. I just wanted her gone. I think it crashed at the bottom somewhere. I thought I could then rush to mother and be given my proper place. It was quite a time before I found her. I think now that she must have been picking up the baby and pram in the meantime. I ran to her glad and happy, but I think she must have seen it happen from a window, for I was simply met by a blizzard, and what can a child do under those circumstances! I was absolutely punctured and deflated. Mother made me good in the end, and now it is imperative that I should give an outlet to my self-assertion or be dead for the rest of my life."

Later he went back to the incident which had occasioned his initial despair on arrival at this session. He said: "I was not in contact with the girl at the time. It was just an upsurge of panic in consequence of my feeling a little self-assertive and having a bit of an erection. It keeps on happening continually. I am striving to feel self-assertion and when it comes I get in a panic and deflate the whole thing. What the hell is the good of me to any man or woman or beast or anything, if I am feeling so deflated!

"Before my mother I was absolutely speechless. That connects up with my being tongue-tied when there is an emotional conflict in me. It is due to the fact that when I was fond of her she turned round and went for me and I was so surprised, I was so hurt at the unexpected and unfair treatment, that I just curled up inside. I can only feel the *final* feelings now and not the original ones."

ANALYST: "*Still, that is some feeling after all.*"

PATIENT: "Yes, it may be feeling, but it is directed inwards instead of outwards."

Whether or not this patient's analytical material gives us some insight into the psychopathology of a very early schizophrenic process, it is certainly suggestive of the early infantile traumatic causes, operating upon a particularly sensitive disposition, which may induce repression of self-assertion, repression of all emotion and absence of affective response and a pretty thorough introversion. It transpired that his almost compulsive behaviour regarding attempts to pick-up strange women was really the

R

actualisation of an infantile compulsion to re-ingratiate himself with his mother, or failing that to show some self-assertion in pursuing his claims. He did not usually succeed in carrying it out in his experimental practice, as the attempt to do so would of course, and did, bring up the infantile conflict instigated by a fear of the "blizzard" or chastisement which such attempts would receive from the mother imago. He himself interpreted it as over-determined, in that it was both an attempt to win mother and to resume his enjoyable play with the little girl of his infancy.

The schizophrenic symptomatology in the form of acts or activities incongruous to his nature, age and status was suggested by the fact that before this interpretation had fully linked up in his mind, he would insist in regarding it as my duty, not to analyse him, but to teach him by encouragement or what-not to overcome his fear of speaking to these strange women and to give him courage to carry out his "self-assertive" acts in reality. This despite the fact that my reply was always to say the acts, ideas or phantasies had no relationship to reality, particularly the reality of the psychology of the women concerned, but were purely and simply nothing more or less than his tendency, through lack of insight, to play out in the present day his infantile struggle to regain his mother's attention. It appears that this was the only residue of "transference" left to support his emotional life.

The importance of transference interpretation as a therapeutic agent in all analyses, even those of narcissistic disorders, is partly revealed by the following excerpt from one of his earlier sessions.

He said: "If I do happen to remember anything of the past while I am in an emotionally repressed state it would be a purely *objective memory* . . . about a little boy whom I know was myself but *do not feel* was myself. Therefore as far as my feeling side is concerned it is quite *unreal*, and that is my present state. My feeling is unreal, is detached from me. The real 'I' is not there. When one says one is emotionally repressed one means the 'I' is emotionally repressed. If I reach an emotional state, it is only then that the 'I' can show itself, that is when the lid can be lifted from the Jack box. This treatment will only help me if you will be prepared not only to discuss some emotional problem that bothers me, but if you will be prepared to make it real to me, because otherwise, unless you can succeed in making it real to me, I have the tendency to put it aside and look upon it objectively as unreal."

It is only when the patient shows affect towards the analyst within the analytical session that the immediate emotional situation is definitely real to him, and it is only by an interpretation of this immediate emotional *transference situation* that he is definitely prevented from objectivising his feeling and adopting this schizophrenic defensive measure of regarding it as a tale that is told about somebody else.

This patient, in spite of his schizophrenic mechanisms, increasingly brought his emotions into the analytical situation as was shown originally by his progressive inability to lie on the settee, and it was particularly the interpretation of transference that made him recognise beyond all shadow of doubt that he was still living his infantile conflict as though in its original setting with his mother. The unreality of his present-day emotional life and his introversion were the direct result of the primitive mental mechanism whereby the child had defended itself against feeling pain, namely, by dissociating all emotional feeling from consciousness. It seems to me that this is probably an important element in initiating the schizophrenic type of reaction—an initial movement which, with the appropriate predisposition, may conceivably progress to the extent of the mental disintegration more readily recognisable as schizophrenia.

The case of the sex-repressed and parent-fixated girl first described, together with this last case, may remind us that it is the Oedipus conflict which leads to such a strong and determined repression of sexuality, extending to all emotions, to the development of introversion in the form of unconscious sexual phantasy and to the consequent dissociation of libido from reality attachment.

Libido cannot reach reality if it is not permitted (on account of persistent Oedipus repression) even to reach consciousness.

Whether or not it subsequently regresses to the first oral stage of libidinal fixation these analytical excerpts do not reveal, but one may say that such a powerful Oedipus (or parental) fixation (particularly as that displayed by our first case with her total sex-repression) is indicative of an equally powerful precursor in the form of the first libidinal fixation to the parent—which of course is oral—in the pattern and intensity of which subsequent libidinal-object patterns must of necessity follow.

Hence we may regard the essential psychological factors initiating a pathological introversion and schizophrenia as those of parent-fixation with consequent repression of sexuality and subsequent regression of libido to early fixation points with a total deflection of it from present-day environment and an absorption of it in archaic unconscious phantasy.

THE SCHIZOPHRENIC REACTION TYPES

Definition. Schizophrenia is a group of reactions characterized by apathetic, silly, or unexpected emotional responses, many types and varieties of defects in the thinking processes, and in most cases the presence of delusional and hallucinatory phenomena.

These reactions were originally grouped together, under the term dementia precox, by Kraepelin because he felt they shared the tendency to chronicity, the tendency to deteriorate and the tendency to develop in early adult life. The present term, schizophrenia, was coined by Bleuler to avoid the unfavorable prognostic implications in the Kraepelinian term, and to more accurately describe the breaking up or dissociation of the normal pattern of response, particularly the disruption, quantitatively, and qualitatively of the usual emotional-ideational parallelism. Adolf Meyer has proposed the term parergasia as a still more accurate expression of the distortions in the behavior pattern seen in this reaction type.

Incidence. Each year, at least 30,000 individuals in the U.S.A. alone develop schizophrenia. Unless treatment is prompt and vigorous these patients become chronic institutional cases, and in too many instances they become chronic in spite of treatment. The age of onset is most often in the late teens or twenties, but cases have been reported as young as six years and as late as 60.

Etiology and Psychopathology. The etiology of the schizophrenic reactions is unknown. In spite of this, less than 1 per cent of the public money spent for the care of these individuals is devoted to research. The theories and explanations of the causes of these reactions are many, and are notable examples of the verbal dexterity of most psychiatrists, but have contributed little to a more satisfactory treatment of the individuals suffering from schizophrenia. The earliest concept that dementia precox was inherited has been largely discarded. Pollock, Malzberg, and Fuller state, "It is clear, therefore, that though there is probably a familial basis for the origin of many cases of mental disorder in the family stock of probands with dementia precox, the observed frequency cannot be described in Mendelian terminology." The theories at present entertained fall into two large groups; (a) That schizophrenia is a functional disorder, a faulty reaction to life experiences with habit deterioration, and (b) That schizophrenia is an organic disease process of unknown cause and unknown pathology.

FUNCTIONAL CONCEPTS. The functional concepts have distinguished American psychiatry under the stimulus of Meyer, Freud, Hoch, White and their pupils. The basic view is that certain individuals meeting life experiences to which they have difficulty in adjusting withdraw or compromise in an unsatisfactory manner. The person finds his satisfaction in phantasy wherein he says or does the things he wished to do in the original setting. Succeeding difficult situations are handled in a similar manner. As time passes and difficulties accumulate, the individual depends to an increasing degree upon himself and his own phantasies for his satisfactions from life. At last a point is reached where these phantasies assume the dominant role in his life and environmental events are interpreted in terms of these phantasies. The patient is said to be living in a world of unreality. His own ideas, wishes and beliefs are attributed to the people in his environment. This results in difficulties in adjustment to family and friends, neglect of business and social obligations, neglect of person, and, at times, conflict with law and social custom. In the longitudinal study of such patients, the step-by-step development of the symptoms and the content of the phantasies and delusions can be understood if the data available is sufficient. This leaves unexplained why the individual reacts in this manner to environmental stresses or even to ordinary environmental expectations. To say it is "a constitutional predisposition" leaves one with another indefinite explanation, and unfortunately, also leaves the question unanswered. One of the marks of predisposition is the so-called "schizoid" temperament.

Bleuler writes of the schizoid as follows: "The schizoid retains his independence towards his surroundings; he strives to withdraw from the affective influences of the living as well as the dead environment and to pursue his own aims. In pathological states this may develop into active, hostile, or passive dereistic[1] (*de reor*, away from reality) attitudes, and in milder forms it still leads to a seclusion from reality or to an active transformation of it for one's own aims, or to an adjustment to reality by means of inventions. The schizoid person may be persecuted or litigious, but he seeks and always finds new paths and outlets . . . the lack of respect for reality and for existing things leads on the one side to an effort to change them somehow, and on the other hand to turn into oneself . . . In contrast to the syntonic (extrovert) who has the ability and will to live through his reactions to outer influences and thus settle them, the schizoid can keep them from discharging, thus saving the motive power for later times and then add it to the feelings tending in the same direction. He thus not only saves force but time and opportunity for reflection and modifications of past inner and outer circumstances."

The schizoid is not in himself mentally abnormal. "Thus, the expression schizoid now designates a type of psychic being and psychic reaction which exists in everyone more or less pronounced, in its morbid aggravation it

[1] "It is characteristic of this 'dereistic thinking' . . . that it totally ignores any contradictions with reality."

manifests itself as schizophrenia, but in its milder development it is seen in the psychopath hitherto designated as schizoid without, however, reaching to the degree of being called a psychotic." (Bleuler.) Nevertheless, the roots of schizophrenia are firmly embedded in schizoid soil.

The person who is schizoid to a dangerous degree does not find the world a pleasant place in which to live. He does not successfully meet reality and his sensitive nature shrinks from "the slings and arrows of outrageous fortune." Secretly, he probably envies success in the abstract, but he hesitates to take the real concrete steps which make for this enviable state. With the dexterity of thought which he possesses he clothes everything in garments of idealism. Sex is beautiful, but its actual physical contacts are not pleasant in his mind. Success in any field is desirable, but competition is distasteful to him. Unquestionably, there is always in his mental life the conflict between the desire to grasp the fruits of endeavor in every phase of life and the shrinking from the bold and positive efforts that must be made before the victory is secured. Without doubt, sooner or later, he comes to the crossroads of his mental life, and there must be some decision as to which path he will tread. Shall he continue the hard battle of facing reality or may he take the easier road? Already he has succumbed to the temptation of excessive daydreaming. It is unreal but pleasing. In this way all the hard knocks of reality are made to disappear and his hurts are soothed.

The schizoid, however, has great capacity for introspection. Thought is at once his greatest security and his greatest danger. One may picture the potential schizophrenic at this stage as courting unreality in his daydreams. If his ultimate fate is to be schizophrenia, he loses some small part of his hold on reality almost day by day. Finally comes the time when, judged by the criterion of the world as applied to himself, the verdict of failure is unescapable. His ego, still strong, cannot accept the conclusion that he did not succeed because, in truth, he could not face the struggle that is necessary.

Theoretically, we are now at the stage where the psychosis is about to come to his rescue. In this connection, it is interesting to note how often the first outspoken symptoms of schizophrenia are, in effect, unconscious and pathologic excuses for the inability to persist in some field of endeavor and overcome the obstacles which are in the way. For instance, in cases A, B, and D to be presented, this phenomenon is strikingly illustrated. When the first case described in this chapter, the medical student, came to the end of his mental string, he suddenly leaned out of the window and screamed loudly—"You dirty s—s of b——s, stop flashing those lights." The second case, the young girl, became "moody," "stared," and went into a panic during which she made a foolish attempt at suicide in the wake of her first and probably only love affair. The third case (p. 279) made a scene in the City Hall because he believed himself persecuted on account of his inventive genius.

We have briefly indicated a few of the preliminary psychologic considerations which seem to underlie the development of schizophrenia. You will recall that first there is a personality, introverted to a dangerous degree. This personality is badly equipped to come to grips with reality. Too often the unsuccessful struggle conditions a retreat and a yearning for that world of unreality and phantasy in which no effort is required to make dreams come true. Eventually, even feeble attempts to dominate the real cease and the break from reality occurs. Since the ego must be absolved, the blame for failure is projected outside the individual onto others or the conditions of things.

The drama of schizophrenia, however, is not yet closed. If this were the end, the patient would immediately retire into the ivory tower of phantasy and would have no more part in the world, as we know it, than if he were actually physically dead. This, of course, is not true; many of the early symptoms bespeak the fact that reality continues to knock at the door of the psychosis. There are panics, suicidal attempts, excitements, and the like. Again, some patients are reclaimed and recover. That means they abandon unreality and become what we call sane.

Various authors divide the psychosis, schizophrenia, into stages which, to our minds, seem artificial and leave out of account the psychopathology. There are only two stages: The first might be called the active stage, and it lasts as long as the patient has not completely accepted the psychotic material. In other words, we may presume that he is still aware, however faintly it may be, of the claims of the real and concrete environment. Once he succeeds in completely shutting this out, he lives wholly in phantasy and has entered the second phase of the psychosis. We speak then of his being deteriorated or even "demented."

The break with the environment lessens the censorship of social criteria, and inhibitions rapidly disappear and uninhibited regressive and primitive speech and forms of behavior are employed to express deeply underlying and often archaic trends.

What of the attitude of the schizophrenic toward environmental reality as the psychosis progresses? We have compared it to the attitude of a man who finds himself at a play which bores him greatly, but he is unable to leave the theater. He has devalued the play, is indifferent to it and escapes by recourse to pleasant and purposeless thinking, but, at least, the potentiality of re-aligning himself with reality remains.

Some psychoanalytic workers have studied schizophrenic patients under analysis. The prolonged study of these cases has led to the conclusion that patients show great difficulty in forming emotional attachments to persons or objects other than themselves. This difficulty in forming a transference to the analyst makes analytic therapy prolonged and at times impossible. The disturbance in the capacity to develop emotional drives or urges toward other persons explains much of the emotional pathology in schizophrenia. The term used to describe this state is "regression to the narcissistic level," and implies that the patient finds satisfaction for his emotional strivings within himself. It also implies that the person has some difficulty in distinguishing between that which is himself and that which is the world about him—a disturbance of ego reference (see Chapter I). The facts are that these theoretical postulates coincide very accurately with the symptomatology seen in schizophrenia and contribute much to our understanding of the symptoms we encounter. Unfortunately we still come back to our first question: Why does the patient do these things in this way? The manner of formation of the symptoms and their meaning can be explained but we do not yet know why the patient has a need to develop an illness to solve his problem. It is a withdrawal from reality, but why does the schizophrenic withdraw?

ORGANIC CONCEPTS. The organic theories have been most popular in Europe. Much material has accumulated, but the findings are inconstant, and in most instances the clinical features of the particular "schizophrenics" studied are not clearly indicated. Many workers have reported a correlation between schizophrenia and the so-called linear or asthenic or leptosomatic body type, but every psychiatrist has seen many typical cases of athletic or pyknic body build. One can say that there are more linear than broad persons suffering from schizophrenia, but body type is apparently not essential to the development of one of this group of disorders.

Pathology in the brain itself has been reported by many laboratory workers. Nissl reports cortical degeneration. Josephy found cellular changes in third and fifth layers of the cortex and Naito confirmed these findings. Funfgeld described lipoid sclerosis in the third cortical layer and lipoid deposits in the optic thalamus. Marcuse claims to have found double nuclei and lipoid degeneration in some of the thalamic ganglion cells. Kitaboyashi reports characteristic changes in the choroid plexus. Alzheimer demonstrated ameboid glia cells in some acute cases. Penfield, and Elvidge and Reed have demonstrated a glial reaction in the white matter of biopsy specimens removed from both acute and chronic cases of schizophrenia. Elvidge and Reed believe the symptoms are due to disturbance of the association pathways, and report similar findings in manic-depressive patients, and patients in a postepileptic stupor. They found no such changes in epileptics who were mentally clear, and no such change in the control patients. Goldstein, Nissl and Orton also found a glial reaction in the white matter and the deep cortical layers plus an increase in the lipoid content of the ganglion cells. Freeman found fat in increased amounts in the cells of the basal ganglia, and calcareous degeneration of the blood vessels in many cases of schizophrenia. Freeman also found a deficiency of iron in the cortical ganglion cells in schizophrenic patients of all types except the paranoid form. Dunlap's famous report did much to discourage further neuropathological studies in America. His report concludes: "For us the changes in the brain of schizophrenia are not only inconstant and non-specific, but they are such as may be found in any series of control cases, in other words, their significance for the disease process seems to be without importance." Many workers, notably Spielmeyer, believe that the pathology is present, but cannot be demonstrated by present laboratory methods. He states "There are many cases in which the anatomical analysis has revealed no deviation from the norm. It does not appear justifiable, however, to conclude, as many investigators have done, that such a negative finding renders apparent the functional rather than the organic nature of the process of dementia praecox."

There are many other studies which show more generalized pathologic and metabolic disturbances. Kraepelin believed that the disease was due to metabolic autointoxication resulting from a disturbance in the gonads. Mott reported testicular and ovarian atrophy with attendant endocrine dysfunction and final brain pathology in schizophrenic patients. This work was severely criticized, and Morse pointed out that the changes were probably unrelated to schizophrenia. Recently Hemphill, Reiss and Taylor report a special form of atrophy of the tubules of the testicles in many schizophrenic patients. They did not encounter these changes in control subjects or in patients suffering from other types of mental disorder. These studies were made on biopsy specimens taken from patients in good physical condition. They found the atrophy varied in severity with the "malignancy of the psychosis," and did not vary with the duration of the illness, the patient's age, or the patient's body type. The atrophy was rare in the paranoid form of schizophrenia, and was never severe in this group. They conclude that the testis change is not the cause of schizophrenia, but is evidence of a complex central imbalance of which it is one sign. "Not related to mental trauma or masturbation." They found the atrophy was not accompanied by a decrease in "17-ketosteroids" or by a loss of secondary sex characteristics. They treated 18 cases with follicle-stimulating gonadotrophic hormone from pregnant mares serum, but the results were not remarkable. Many other laboratory findings of interest have been reported; Kasanin noted a high sustained glucose curve during stupor; Whitehorn noted decreased glucose tolerance and diminished inorganic phosphates in the blood plasma; Hertz found shortening of blood coagulation time; Bowman reported evidence of polyglandular disorder; Henry found definite changes in gastrointestinal motor function, especially in acute cases, similar to those associated with fear or rage; Malamud and Rothchild found decreased permeability to bromides of the blood cerebrospinal fluid barrier in 60 per cent of schizophrenic subjects; Wikoff, Martin and Marvin found the bromine content of the blood lower in schizophrenic patients than in control subjects living in the same city and drinking water from the same source; Freidman, Emerick and Thale report a smaller rise in cerebrospinal fluid pressure, from histamine injections, in schizophrenic patients than in their control series; Katzenelbogen, Solomon and Snyder found serum potassium elevated in five patients in a group of 29 schizophrenics studied, and state the variation is due to emotional states; Harris found 33 per cent of his schizophrenic patients had serum with a "pronounced antagonistic effect on the action of insulin," but could note no correlation between the symptoms and the presence of abnormal reaction to insulin; Meduna first found this abnormal reaction to insulin in 60 per cent of his schizophrenic patients; Molholm found, in a series of 12 schizophrenic patients, that his subjects did not develop sensitivity to guinea-pig serum as readily as control subjects.

STUDIES ON THE GLUCOSE AND OXYGEN METABOLISM IN SCHIZOPHRENIA. Recently Meduna has shown that the changes in the blood chemical constituents, particularly in the glucose and carbohydrate metabolism is identical in the various types of shock therapy. He concludes that the shock treatments bring about a condition which interfered with the enzyme system in carbohydrate metabolism. In regards to the biochemical changes in the brain itself, it has been demonstrated that the pH of the cortex shows similar alkaline shift in both hypoglycemic and convulsive treatment, and an acid shift during the period of relative anoxia. Lactic acid and phosphorus increase during both convulsions and anoxia. An increase of inorganic phosphorus explains itself by a decrease of phosphocreatine. A relative anoxia of the cortex appears before, during, and after convulsions, and a similar condition prevails during anoxemia. The production of acetylcholine is decreased in hypoglycemia and anoxia. It seems that any means of treating schizophrenic conditions must interfere with some phase of the carbohydrate metabolism if it is to be effective. At present we do not know just how this disturbance must be brought about but it seems necessary to interfere in some manner with carbohydrate and oxygen metabolism in order to bring about any therapeutic effect in schizophrenia.

Lewis and his workers at Columbia have done much work on the constitutional factors in schizophrenia. They have found that the average heart size in hebephrenic and catatonic schizophrenic patients is on the average smaller than in other mental disorders, and smaller than the published figures for the average normal human. They also found that the testes, the thyroid, and adrenal glands were rather small in the schizophrenic patients. They postulate some defect in the growth processes as playing a role in schizophrenia. In terms of the constitutional factors in schizophrenia there have been several reports on twins. Recently Arieti made a report on a pair of monozygotic twins in which the most asthenic, more passive and less well adjusted one developed the illness first, had projections and became chronic. The one who had a more athletic habitus handled problems better and had more neurotic complaints of a somatic type, recovered promptly. One wonders in this case whether the second one might not have represented an example of folie à deux phenomena.

One of the most conclusive studies indicating the presence of a strong genetic or constitutional factor in schizophrenia is the study performed by Kallman and the following information was furnished to us through the courtesy of Nolan Lewis and Francis J. Kallman. The conclusions are based on 794 sets of twins, and 691 families of twins, which included 2,741 full siblings, 134 half-siblings, 74 step-siblings, 1,191 parents and 264 marriage partners of twin patients. The morbidity rate discovered in this series is in line with a genetic theory of schizophrenia. They found an incidence of 1.8 per cent with schizophrenia in step-siblings, 2.1 per cent for the marriage partners, 7.0 per cent for the half-siblings, 9.2 per cent for the parents, 14.3 per cent for the full-siblings, 14.7 per cent for the dizygotic co-twins and 85.8 per cent for the monozygotic co-twins. "This morbidity distribution indicates that the chance of developing schizophrenia in comparable environment increases in proportion to the degree of blood relationship with schizophrenic index case." The data has been presented in great detail by Dr. Kallman and the student is referred to it. It is emphasized by Kallman and Lewis in their report that the genetic theory does not invalidate any psychologic theory of a descriptive or analytic nature and is equally compatible with the psychiatric concept that schizophrenia may be prevented as well as cured. It is, however, the most definite evidence yet published as to the presence of a genetic factor in schizophrenic cases.

Symptomatology: History Summary. One of the most characteristic findings in schizophrenia is the history of the patient's development. In the majority of cases the childhood will be characterized by difficulty in socialization with other children. The inability to find a workable means of forming friendships, giving and receiving satisfactions in play, winning and losing his own battles, expanding his contacts with people and resources in his environment results in unhappiness, feelings of inadequacy and finally withdrawal from an active participation in the community life of his playmates. Attempts to compensate and find satisfaction in adult approval frequently make these children well behaved, quiet, and studious. At times these efforts are successful and the child is regarded as precocious or brilliant by his parents and teachers. His playmates usually regard him as "queer," "a sissy," "teacher's pet," or "an icky." With time this leads to more and more withdrawal, and increasing dependence upon daydreaming, and later phantasy for the satisfaction of the drives finding no outlet in the environment. Then the child may be described by parents as "lazy," "daydreamy," "stubborn," or "stupid." His school work suffers and in some instances these youngsters are removed from school because of "nervousness." The development of interest in the opposite sex at puberty is characterized by phantasies and masturbation rather than efforts at social contacts and sex play directed toward the available persons of the opposite sex, and with masturbation often the sole substitute. It is often difficult or impossible to determine just when the psychotic phase begins. In some instances the family will report a sudden onset with hallucinations or the free expression of delusions. In many cases, more careful inquiry will divulge an in-between period of peculiar and bizarre ideas, periods of confusion, and periods of very rich and vivid phantasy preceding the time of onset as fixed by the family. In some instances this general type of history is not found. This may be an example of a mother's projection of her ambitions rather than the facts of the history, but in some instances it is accurate. In such cases, the early ability to establish good emotional relationship to the environment is a favorable prognostic sign. If chronologic adulthood is reached prior to the onset of symptoms, the history often reveals a failure to assume adult responsibilities. They are often dependent upon others for emotional support, usually single, and if married, dependent upon the spouse for support and mothering. Any skill or achievement reached is usually in the intellectual or cultural fields, where mutually satisfactory emotional relationships with their fellow creatures are not necessary for success.

PHYSICAL SUMMARY. There are no specific physical or neurologic abnormalities in schizophrenia. Many patients show evidence of poor vasomotor control manifest by peripheral cyanosis of a peculiar mottled type, localized edema, localized sweating, abscence of pupillary response to emotion, and hypotension. Secondary infections, anemias, poor nutrition, poor gastrointestinal function and like dysfunctions are frequently encountered and are probably due to neglect and lack of proper hygienic care.

MENTAL SUMMARY. The mental symptoms in schizophrenia vary greatly in individual patients, yet they share in common certain types of emotional change and distortions in thinking which Bleuler considers the basic or primary symptoms, and most patients experience delusional and hallucinatory phenomenon, which are the most spectacular part of the illness.

SYMPTOMS MANIFEST BY DISTURBANCE IN BEHAVIOR. The behavior of persons suffering from schizophrenia is usually distinguished by some unusual feature. The most typical behavior is that of shyness, the desire to be alone, active avoidance of friends and family, and a tendency to stand, sit or lie for long periods lost in phantasy—known to students as "schizing"—and oblivious of the environmental events about them. In some patients this preöccupation becomes very pronounced and the patient appears to be in a stupor, responding only to acutely painful stimuli. In severe cases, they are said to have developed "catatonia" and some of them may be placed in awkward, uncomfortable or ridiculous positions which they will maintain for long periods of time. Such a state, called "waxy flexibility" or "cataleptic" is associated with drooling of the saliva, retention or incontinence of feces and urine, and failure to take food or fluids voluntarily. Failure to move about for longperiods results in postural edema, and in these cases a peculiar mottled type of peripheral cyanosis is often encountered. Patients with catatonic symptoms may show short periods of overactivity during which they fight, assault other patients and personnel, disrobe and break up the furnishings in their room. After a period of overactivity, which may vary from a few minutes to several weeks, they return to their lethargic semistuporous or stuporous state. Other patients may be overactive in a silly facetious way. They dance, sing, and go through weird and intricate gestures, all of which symbolize or act out of portions of their phantasies and delusions. Some of this group decorate themselves with trash, rags, jewelry or anything available as part of their symbolization. Others draw, paint, carve, or model intricate abstract designs and stylized figures as part of their symbolization. In the paranoid form of schizophrenia, the patient's behavior may attract little attention. Many carry on their daily activity in a satisfactory fashion, but close scrutiny will usually disclose bizarre diaries and other unusual written productions, hidden "evidence" of their persecution, often protected by elaborate precautions, duplicate copies, lock-boxes, etc. They may have elaborate systems of lights, escape routes, and at times dictaphone recorders as self-protective devices. These anomalies of behavior may be concealed for long periods by these patients, and they are disclosed with great reluctance in many cases. Homicidal assaults occur in some instances, but much less frequently than the general public believes. These aggressive acts may occur during bursts of catatonic excitement mentioned above, as part of the acting out of phantasies of a religious sort, as a result of orders and commands received via their hallucinatory experiences, or to protect themselves from imagined dangers or threats.

Symptoms Manifest by Disturbance in Thinking. Disturbances in thinking are characteristic of schizophrenia, and occur in all cases. Bleuler, with many others, believe that these disturbances are fundamental symptoms. These disturbances or distortions are of several types, all more or less related. Disorders of content are found in most schizophrenic cases. These are manifest by the delusions, peculiar beliefs and bizarre ideas encountered in these cases. Because of their unusual nature, these ideas are most easily detected, and are the ones associated with "insanity" in the average lay persons thinking. Disorders of form and organization are more difficult to detect but are even more specific for the schizophrenic group of disorders than the content disturbance.

concrete *vs.* conceptual thinking. Goldstein has described the thinking in schizophrenia as "concrete" as opposed to "conceptual" in normals. By concrete thinking, he means the interpretation of words, and environmental activity in terms of one's own associations or phantasies at the moment. Events of any sort are interpreted, not in the setting in which they occur, but in terms of one's own phantasies, or thoughts at the moment they occur. An example would be: a patient thinking that his fellow patients dislike him hears another patient sneeze. Instead of believing that the other patient had a cold or some other nasal irritation, the schizophrenic patient interprets the sneeze as an insulting gesture performed to annoy him, and he may even think it symbolizes or means the other patient regards him as a homosexual or a s.o.b. Another example would be a patient who believes he is Jesus. This idea persists in spite of the fact that he is in a hospital with few privileges and no power to alter his own living arrangements.

dissociated thinking. In so-called normal thinking a person constantly chooses from an immense number of possible associations that have been created by the individual's past experience. The final selection is guided by the goal idea, modified by affect, and finally organized according to the person's concept of the situation. For example, if I am in the surgery and think of alcohol I then associate it with dressings, cleansing of skin, etc., but if at a party, the associations are of drinking, past indulgences and the gregarious pleasures associated with intoxication. In the schizophrenias the associations no longer follow ordinary channels toward a final goal but may suddenly leave the primary topic and wander off on some irrelevant byway. The classic example is the schizophrenic patient who, when asked the question: "Who was Brutus?," answered "Brutus was an Italian." In his answer the patient displays an understanding of the problem and gave the right association to place, but failed in the time association. Still more advanced cases show a complete lack of sequence and are not associated with anything apparent. Example: I went for a walk. God is in me. They say I am immoral. Nurse, nurse, nurse. Where is my baby?

COMBINING OR FUSING IDEAS THAT HAVE NO LOGICAL CONNECTION. This symptom is occasionally seen in advanced schizophrenia and is similar to some of the false or chance associations reproduced in the speech of children. For example, a patient sitting alone laughing was asked why he laughed, responded "because you are a doctor," in spite of the fact that he was laughing prior to your appearance. Another example is the patient who knows the doctor is married and the nurse is married and assumes that they are man and wife.

CONDENSATION. Several different ideas may be combined in a process called condensation. The Bleulerian example is the patient who sees a steamer and sailboat and speaks of "Steamsails."

DISPLACEMENT OF IDEAS IN WHICH ONE IDEA APPEARS FOR ANOTHER. This situation is seen in the productions of schizophrenics and in certain psychoneurotics. An example was seen in a patient, Mrs. Smith, who had been mistreated by an instructor while a student nurse. In the hospital in which she is a patient there is a nursing instructor who remotely resembles the patient's former teacher. The patient attacked the instructor at every opportunity, but coöperated well with the other nurses on the floor.

SYMBOLIZATION. Symbolization is a special form of displacement and is frequently used by schizophrenics on occasions where the ordinary person would have expressed the real idea. Bleuler's example is the pregnant schizophrenic who expressed the fact that she was pregnant by stating: "I hear a stork clapping in my body." Another example is speaking of impending death as "the hovering of angels." In the schizophrenic, the symbol takes the place of the original idea unnoticed by the patient.

VAGUENESS AS OPPOSED TO THE CONCRETE. General vague notions are utilized where a concrete statement would be the expected reply. An example is the schizophrenic's explanation for a quarrel with an attendant over a cigarette, "Because I hate to be in the hospital." Here the general unrest at confinement is given as the specific cause for some inappropriate action.

MEDIATE ASSOCIATIONS. Mediate associations are often found in association tests in schizophrenics. Example (from Bleuler): To the stimulus "wood" the patient responded "cousin." This because his cousin was dead and buried in a wooden coffin.

LACK OF A CENTRAL IDEA OR "SKIDDING." Patient's productions are such that neither the patient nor the physician know why such ideas are expressed. The train of thought sometimes resembles a flight of ideas, but the absence of an objective becomes noticeable through the lack of emotional tone. In a true flight of ideas, an objective is present, but this objective is frequently changed due to external or internal stimuli. The objective is also clothed with the appropriate affect in a true flight of ideas. Bleuler's example of skidding is the essay "Blossom-Time for a Horticulturist" which is reproduced in part:

> At the time of the New-Moon, Venus stands in the August heavens of Egypt and with its rays of light illuminates the harbors of commerce, Suez, Cairo, and Alexandria. In this historically famous city of the Kalifs, there is situated in the museum of Assyrian monuments from Macedonia. There plantain flourishes next to maize columns, oats, clover, and barley, also bananas, figs, lemons, oranges, and olives. Olive oil is an Arbian liqueur-sauce, with which Afghans, Moors, and Moslemites carry on the breeding of ostriches. . . . "

CIRCUMSTANTIALITY. A frequent change in the direction of the train of thought, but the goal idea is maintained and ultimately reached. There are numerous digressions, but the general pathway of the story is incapable of distinguishing between essentials and nonessentials, and thus must go into unimportant details as fully as into the main issues. This condition is found in schizophrenics and organic psychoses, being especially common in the senile states.

GENERALIZATIONS. In this symptom a thought which logically applies to one person or subject is applied generally. An example would be a schizophrenic who felt that every reference to the color red implied prostitution and was an invitation for coitus. This symptom resembles the stage of generalization of associations seen in the very young child.

IMPAIRMENT OF LOGICAL OR NORMAL ASSOCIATIONS. Example: To the test "Two children fell into the river. One was rescued and one was . . . ?," a schizophrenic responded "saved."

OBSTRUCTION OR DEPRIVATION OF THOUGHT, BLOCKING. The patients may say that their thoughts are drawn away from them by some outside force. In this condition the progression of thought stands still for a short period of time, and the patient can find no cause within himself, so he projects it to some outside force. The obstruction may last for a few minutes or many hours. When the obstruction is over, a new thought, which had no connection with the obstruction, may appear. For example, a schizophrenic who is asked, "Where is your wife?," responds "My wife is . . . " and is unable to go on. After a few moments of sterile effort he may continue feebly with "she works." A physical analogy would be the sudden closing of a valve on a stream of water. When the obstruction disappears, the stream of thought goes on as freely as before.

BREVITY OF ASSOCIATIONS AND IMPOVERISHED THINKING. This occurs in many cases. In this phenomena the patient is satisfied with an abbreviated thought without carrying it on to its logical conclusion. For example, a patient reads a fable but cannot repeat it unless prompted step by step. Or when asked to tell of his divorce a patient answered only "I am divorced." Why? "She ran away." Why? "We didn't get along." etc. This symptom also resembles many of the egocentric productions of the child, but probably differs in the affect present.

PERSEVERATION. Perseveration is the persistent repetition of one word or group of words, in spite of the individual's attempt to change the topic, and the observer's attempt to introduce other stimuli. For example, a patient is asked how old he is and answers, "I'm 28." He then continues to repeat "I'm 28" to subsequent questions in spite of his effort to answer relevantly. In most cases the answer was relevant to the original question but bears no relation to the succeeding ones. This occurs in many organic cases and in some of the advanced schizoid disorders.

NEOLOGISMS. Neologisms sometimes occur. They are words of the patient's own making and are often condensations of several other words. Originally they have special meaning for the patient. An unusual example of this is the so-called "Quintalk" of the Dionne children which is a language they have developed for themselves and which they alone understand. Another example is a patient who felt that he had special powers due to "stagnatic electricity" in his body.

RAMBLING. This is very common. Garrulous patients will relate a long story, mixing heterogeneous portions with no attempt to combine them into a concise story. There is an apparent loss of the goal idea. For example, a patient tells of his travels, his work, and his numerous marriages, without any attempt to weld it into a coherent account of where he has been or what he has seen.

OMISSIONS. Omissions are seen, the patient leaving out a significant phrase or sentence in his expression of an idea. For example, a patient states, "The train came roaring down the track. . . . Forty persons were killed." He omits the significant sentence, "A portion of track was washed away in a flood and the train was wrecked."

PSEUDOPROFUNDITY. Often pseudoprofundity is seen and consists of simple thoughts expressed in aphorisms, poetry, etc. For example, a patient who wished to say that his parents did not get along together stated. "They get along like sulfuric acid and sodium hydroxide," or one who described his wife as "more beautiful than the temples of Rome, and more imposing than Gibraltar."

ASYNDETIC THINKING (CAMERON). Asyndetic thinking is a lack of integration of speech, ideas that are relevant are grouped together without any attempt to make a logical connection between them. For example, a patient says "The wind blows because it is time to blow." "The sky makes it blow."

"Because it is high in the air." Similar examples of this reasoning are seen in the child in the prelogical phase, and in this sphere are referred to as juxtapositions.

METONYMIC DISTORTIONS (CAMERON). These are felt to be due to faulty concept formation. In this symptom the patient fails to make a precise choice of term with the result that the expression is only an approximation of the original theme and requires translation. For example, a patient states his body makes a shadow "because it hides the part of the light that is used for full room capacity or area capacity which you intervene."

There are undoubtedly other examples of disorders of the thinking processes but familiarity with the above material will greatly expand one's field of examination and increase his understanding of the behavior and activity of the psychotic patient.

The examination for thinking disorders may be conducted in a variety of ways. Various authors have offered cleverly devised tests in which one must associate likes and differences of figures. Some are more complex and require the formation of new concepts before the proper association can be made. Other tests use proverb interpretations, incomplete sentences, word definitions, word associations, and simple problems in logic as the basis for the test situation. All of these procedures are helpful, but they all share a common defect to a varying degree; that is, the psychotic who is only moderately disorganized is able to meet the test situation and gives the usual "normal" response to the test, because he appreciates the test situation and has enough preservation of affect to make every effort to meet it adequately. The same patient in spontaneous conversation, or in a question-answer interview may show a wealth of material representative of disordered thought, probably because in this latter situation he is rather indifferent to the reaction of his audience. We have had success in demonstrating these aberrations in the phenomenon of thinking in the patient's spontaneous conversation and in essays or letters to relatives, as well as by use of any of the more formal tests. The Rorschach experiment also demonstrates disorders in thinking.

SYMPTOMS MANIFEST BY CHANGES IN EMOTIONAL RESPONSE. The changes in emotional response are another prominent feature of schizophrenic disorders and Bleuler considers these changes, plus the disorders in thinking, as the primary or basic symptoms. The emotional response is usually inadequate, the patient being apathetic or relatively indifferent to the emotion-producing events in his environment. This indifference is sometimes called emotional blunting or "planed off" affect. At times the emotional response is inappropriate or concretely schizophrenic, the patient laughing at sad stimuli, etc. In many patients the emotions are mixed and the patient cannot seem to decide whether to be angry, happy, or sad, and this perplexity and indecision or equal weighting is called ambivalence. When the emotional reaction is inappropriate to his ideas or thoughts at a given moment, it is spoken of as a dissociated affect. All of these changes are described in terms of the examiner's ideas, beliefs, and feelings. The patient's behavior becomes more understandable if we consider the reasons for it. In this disorder, the patient has ceased looking to his environment for either emotional stimuli or satisfaction. He has, in the course of development of his illness, become almost wholly dependent upon himself for emotional satisfaction. He realizes his ambitions and fulfills his desires on an autistic level, and having found these satisfactions within himself he has little need or desire to please or be pleased by the persons in his environment. This results in seeming apathy and indifference to the people about him. The inappropriate affect is often understandable if one considers that the patient has his own special concept of the situation, and his smile on receiving word of a relative's death may be prompted by his belief that this note is proof of his power and that the death occurrred because he wished it to be so. Other patients seem to be under a great emotional strain or tension. This is manifest by sweating, sighing and motor restlessness. At times the tension is discharged in homicidal or destructive outbursts that are unprovoked by the environment, violent, and usually of short duration. As a rule one finds the tension is secondary to the ideas and delusions the patient is entertaining, but in others the reason is deeper and eludes detection. Patients with this type of emotional reaction are usually in the acute phase, and with chronicity and institutional care, most of them develop the characteristic apathy, failing to respond even to their own phantasies. Patients in the paranoid group show less disturbance in the emotional reactions than the other forms of schizophrenia, but some distortion appears in all cases.

Symptoms Manifest by Special Preoccupations, Hallucinations, and Delusions. These special trend reactions are so frequent in schizophrenia and so far removed from normal human experience that their presence is sometimes thought to be specific for the schizophrenic group of disorders. This is not true, however, and while these symptoms do reach their ultimate in chronicity, absurdity, and bizarrity in the schizophrenias, yet they are encountered in many other psychotic reactions. Many patients suffering from this illness are suspicious, feel they are misunderstood and mistreated. Many have definite persecutory ideas, feeling that various fraternal, political, religious, or family groups are organized to persecute, harass, and harm them. Some believe they are being gassed, poisoned, hypnotized or influenced by radio, television, or by God. Others interpret innocent actions of other persons as referring to them specifically, so-called "ideas of reference," and offer an excellent example of the concrete thinking described by Goldstein. Many patients have passivity feelings, believing they must do as the "voices" tell them, and disclaiming any personal responsibility for their thoughts, words, or actions. Hallucinations are common in schizophrenia, being found in 60 to 70 per cent of these patients. Auditory hallucinations are the more commonly encountered, but they may involve any of the sensory fields. The content of the hallucination is colored by the patient's preoccupations, education, and past experience, and represents a projection of his phantasies and desires

Some patients in this group have weird, somatic delusions, believing their organs are gone, feeling electricity in their body, having intercourse by remote control, and similar silly ideas.

Symptoms Manifest by Defects in Intellectual Resources. The intellectual reactions are not seriously impaired in schizophrenia. The changes present are more apparent than real and are due to inattention and indifference rather than to loss of capacity. The judgment is impaired in terms of the disturbance in emotion, thinking, and the imaginary experiences. Most of these patients have little insight, failing to understand that the beliefs and experiences which are so vivid to them, are peculiar to themselves and lack meaning to other people. In the early phases, some patients realize they are undergoing some serious mental disturbance. They may seek aid at this time and if they do it is the optimum time for treatment. In this initial stage, some patients become worried over these mental changes, become depressed in reaction to them, and at this time may commit suicide. In most cases, however, the transition to acceptance of a belief in their symptoms is accomplished smoothly and the things we call delusions, imaginations, and so forth, represent the facts of reality to the patient.

It is customary to divide the schizophrenias into four groups, originally described by Kraepelin, but the student is advised to avoid hairsplitting attempts to differentiate these subgroups too rigidly. There is probably quite a gulf between the paranoid and the other forms, but by and large one is apt to find hebephrenic, catatonic, and paranoid symptoms in a vast majority of schizophrenics. In the *simple* type interest is at a low ebb. There is apathy and strange behavior, and delusions and hallucinations are either abortive and fragmentary or absent entirely; in *hebephrenia*, usually beginning at an early age, there is silliness, unexplained smiling, laughing, grimacing, mannerisms, and peculiar and changeable ideas which are absurd and grotesque; in *catatonia*, usually beginning a bit later than hebephrenia, there is negativism and conduct peculiarity with phases of stupor or excitement, marked by impulsive, queer, stereotyped behavior, and hallucinations; in the paranoid type, averaging much later in life in its onset than the other forms, and occurring as late as 40 or even later, there are delusions, particularly of persecution or of grandeur, often moderately well systematized for a time at least, and hallucinations.

The following cases illustrate the foregoing material and are typical of the variety of schizophrenic symptoms seen in any psychiatric clinic. The first two cases illustrate the history of patients who develop schizophrenia. They are also good examples of patients who have a mixture of catatonic and paranoid symptoms with rich hallucinatory and delusional content.

This young man is 30 years old. One maternal uncle committed suicide in middle life but otherwise his family history is negative. His mother, who gave the history, described him as a quiet and "good" baby and child. During his 'teens he was shy, diffident, and reserved; did not like athletics, read a great deal, liked to be alone in his room, was painfully awkward and embarrassed at parties, and was afraid of girls. He did exceedingly well in his studies and had excellent grades in high school and college. In college he had no friends excepting his roommate. He wanted to study medicine, and in 1924 was admitted to a Class A Medical School. His first year was uneventful. Apparently, the second year was hard for him. He complained that the work was difficult, developed headaches, could not concentrate, and lost weight. He said several of his professors had "it in for him" and had him "spotted for a flunk."

One night, while alone in his room in a students' boarding house, studying for final examinations, he suddenly leaned out of the window and screamed loudly "You dirty s__s of b____s, stop flashing that light in my eyes." Then he was brought to the psychopathic pavilion.

He has many of the classical symptoms of schizophrenia. Often he is mute, but from time to time he will talk in a fragmentary manner about his persecutors. He calls them "mentalists." They disarranged his thoughts so that he could not study medicine. They call him vile names—"dirty dog," "sex pervert," etc. At night they direct a powerful "N Ray" at him and rob him of his semen, etc. You will note that as he speaks of these happenings, he is little or not at all disturbed emotionally. He is not angry or violent or even worried, as one would expect a man to be who believed himself subjected to abuse, torture, and persecution. Often he simpers in a silly fashion; there have been several periods of catatonia during which he was mute, made no response to pin-pricks, had to be fed with a nasal tube, and would retain his limbs in awkward positions for long periods of time.

You have observed that his coat is decorated with odds and ends of brightly colored trash. On his head he wears an old overseas cap with a tin gilt star pinned to it. Occasionally, he raises his right arm extending the index finger. From the notes it appears that this indicates that he is "the Highest Potent." In spite of this he does various odd chores about the ward and is not above retrieving and smoking half-consumed cigarettes.

The second patient is a young woman, 23 years old. Her father was a ne'er-do-well who served several short sentences in the county jail for various minor offenses. Finally, he was shot and killed in a street brawl. Her mother and two brothers and one sister are plain, uneducated, honest, hard-working people.

Her mother tells us she was always a "good" girl but very different from her sister who liked boys and parties. Mary, the patient, was always serious and "worrisome." In school she studied hard and "fussed" about her lessons. She went to church a great deal and was very conscientious. She was meticulously neat and clean and modest and did not even like her sister to see her unless she was completely clothed.

As a child she was not given any sex information and was not prepared for the first menstrual period. When this appeared she was greatly upset and felt that she had "sinned."

She worked in a stocking factory and did routine work well. She wanted to do better, however, and in addition to her work she went to night school. This she had to abandon because of poor health. She was bitterly disappointed and called herself a "failure."

She did not get on well with the other girls in the factory. They thought she was "high hat." She did not "know how to talk to them" and was shy and often painfully embarrassed when they discussed their boy friends or told off-color stories. She had an acne skin eruption and thought "the girls talked about it."

Her mother states that "Mary wanted the boys to like her and wanted to be nice to them but did not know how." Her sister teased her about this. One young man did seem to be very fond of her and called a number of times to see her. Following his last visit, Mary became "moody," spoke very infrequently, "stared," and occasionally smiled without reason. One afternoon, soon after returning from work, she went into the bathroom, took off all her clothing, and lightly gashed her wrist with one of her brother's discarded razor blades. Then she began to scream and continued to scream for 15 minutes. Her mother came to her assistance and she was brought to the psychopathic pavilion. This was seven months ago. Soon after admission she became catatonic and for two months was mute and had to be tube-fed. She was often untidy and would lie on the floor with her arms outstretched in the shape of a cross. Occasionally she emitted piercing screams and once talked in a high-pitched voice for about 30 minutes, scolding, and apparently answering voices.

During the past few months she has been quiet. The most frequently occurring adjectives in the nurses' description notes is "silly." Hour after hour she smiles in a foolish, vapid manner. Sometimes she whispers and when the words can be distinguished, they are "Queen of Heaven"—"Heavenly Lover"—"Immaculate Conception."

She does not show any interest in occupation in the shop but helps carry trays in the ward.

The third case is an example of paranoid schizophrenia and is presented in some detail because it illustrates a characteristic developmental history, the prepsychotic personality pattern, and a characteristic fairly well-organized delusional system seen in this type of reaction. The symbolic activity is illustrated and interpreted by the patient in the accompanying photographs.

About March 1921, the patient complained of hearing voices talking to him. Patient said that these voices were "razzing him" in English, and a man named F. was "tutoring him" in German. He averred that two men, McC. and F., led the Detective Bureau to watch his movements continuously. Frequently remarked that he was under the influence of electric machines which kept "boosting" him up and down. He thought that at times his body was full of electricity. For eight months the voices have been changed, they refer to his wife, frequently call him a "poor simp" because he did not "get wise" to his wife sooner, and because he did not know "there was an organization working directly against him." This organization operated through the Detective Bureau according to the patient's statement. In the afternoon of the day of his admission he created a disturbance in City Hall, demanding to see one of the judges in order to get justice and was very threatening. Stated that if he could not get justice here he would go to the Department of Justice in Washington and see the President.

PERSONAL HISTORY. Normal birth and development. Born June 14, 1882. Had the usual childhood diseases with no sequelae. No serious accidents or operations. Patient began school at the age of five, got along very well, graduating from High School at the age of 17. After graduation from High School he went to work at architecture and civil engineering. He always held very good positions with good salary since he was considered capable and efficient. His habits were normal as far as could be discovered. Patient was married when he was 23 years old and has two children who are now 12 and 14 years of age. He was always jealous and suspicious of his wife, frequently accusing her of receiving attentions from other men. These difficulties increased until May 1920, when his wife left him and has since refused to live with him.

GENERAL MAKE-UP. The patient was always considered to be a very keen, intelligent, but suspicious type of individual. He frequently showed this suspicion in his work by complaining to his fellow associates that his ability was not recognized. He was always distrustful of his superiors and would have been discharged if his

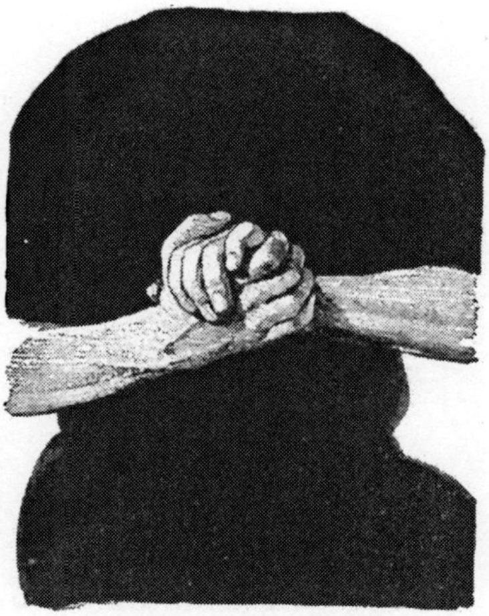

FIG. 18. Physical brotherhood.

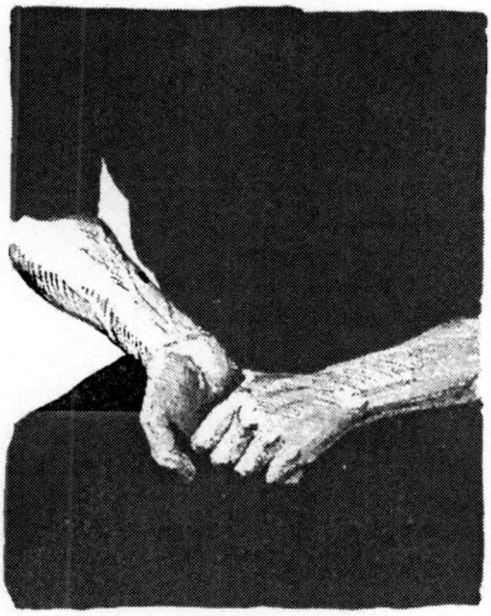

FIG. 19. Spiritual brotherhood. Differs from Fig. 18—the palm of the right hand being turned outward, fingers grasped in the left hand.

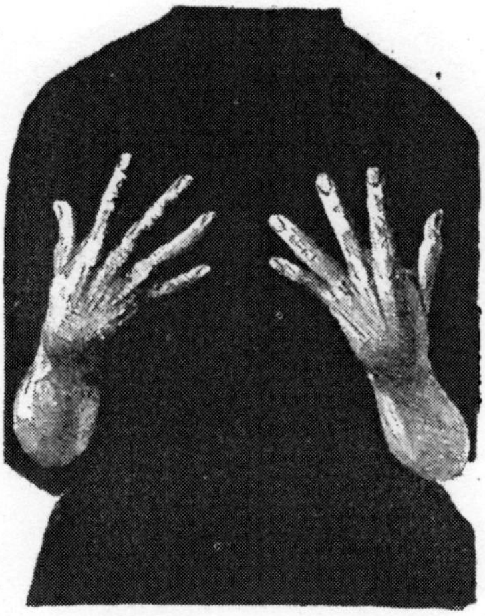

FIG. 20. The ten commandments shown by spreading out the fingers wide and held away from the body.

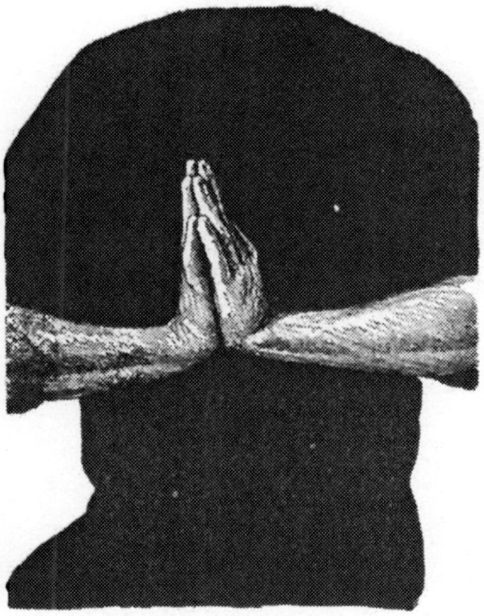

FIG. 21. Usually succeeds.

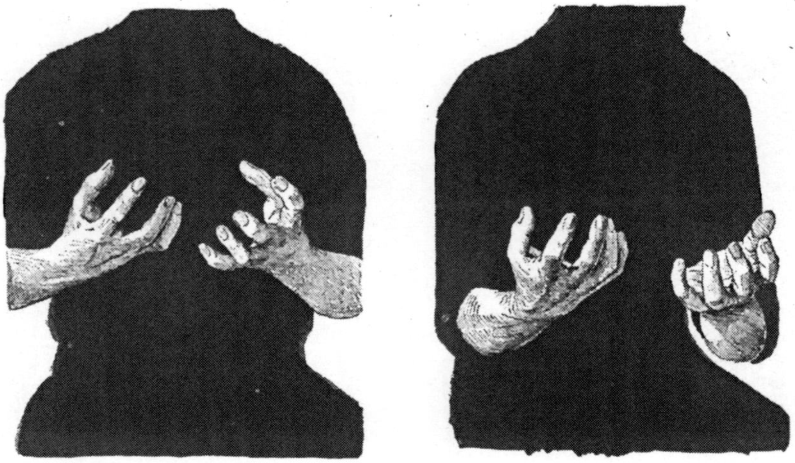

FIG. 22. (*Left*) Spirit of God coming in. The hands held in a receptive posture. (*Right*) Spirit of God going out.

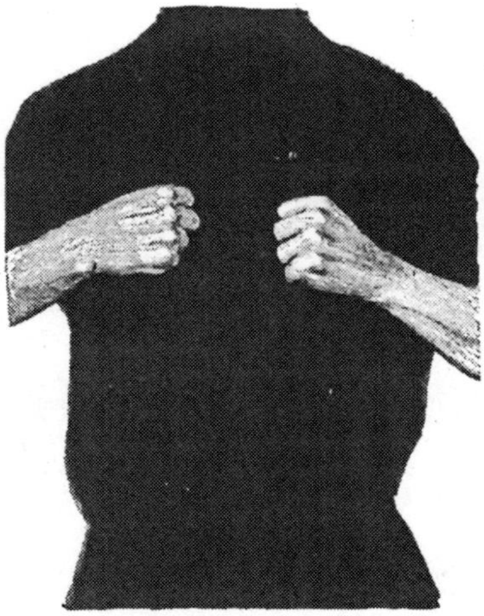

FIG. 23. We must all pull together—unity. Arms tense, muscles quivering, patient pulling his arms apart.

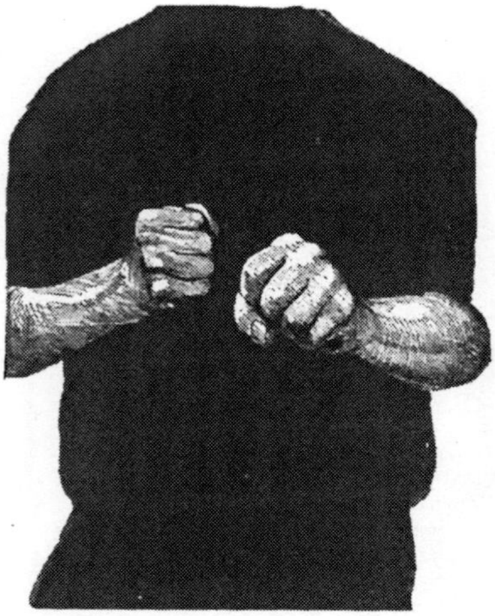

FIG. 24. Power. Determined by a lateral motion of arms like a driving rod.

work had not been so efficient. His fellow associates considered him a very odd, erratic, peculiar type of individual, and by some he was considered a genius.

FAMILY HISTORY. Father died at the age of 50 from pneumonia. Mother is living and well. She is considered to be a highly nervous woman but has had no definite breakdowns. Three brothers and three sisters are living and well. No history of any mental disease in the family.

MENTAL EXAMINATION: *General Behavior*. Patient was very suspicious, keen and alert. His demeanor was self-assertive and he was inclined to be antagonistic and surly. He demanded his immediate freedom and was very belligerent towards the physicians who admitted him.

Stream of Talk and Activity. Talk was spontaneous but guarded, irrelevant, and incoherent. He uttered neologisms, such as, "People are torturing me. I must follow the lead. People are razzing me." Patient said that this trouble had been going on for many years.

Mood and Special Preöccupation. Patient's mood was inadequate. Despite the seriousness of his persecutory ideas, he did not appear to be much troubled by them. Paranoid delusions were prominent and were directed against the two men, McC. and F. of the Detective Bureau, whom he thought had been following him for six to eight months, hounding him from place to place, and continuously on his trail. They have tried to do away with him; have tried to dope him; have set his wife against him; and now that his money is gone, they want to arrest him and place him behind bars for life. He stated that he had tried in many ways to avoid these men, that he has gone to New York, Boston, and Baltimore and Washington without being able to get rid of them. They spread various reports about him, particularly about his character and his treatment of his wife, etc. On close questioning the patient stated that this had been going on for the past eight years, but it had become especially troublesome eight months ago. Then he felt that things had "come to a head," so he bought a revolver and made plans to protect himself either by taking the law in his hands or by having legal proceedings instituted against these men and the organization that they were leading against him. He could assign no definite reason for his persecution.

Hallucinations. Patient heard voices talking to him. The voices are chiefly those of McC. and F. who "razz him and torture him." They refer to intimate affairs with his wife, make fun of him in various ways, say that they will get him. The patient denied hallucinations in the visual field.

Ideas of Influence. Present and prominent. Felt he was under the influence of electric machines, including x-ray machines, induction coils, etc. "Electricity goes through my body."

Sensorium and Intellectual Resources. Patient was oriented for time, place, and person. He had a fair knowledge of current events and his memory was very good for both remote and recent events. His grasp of general information was excellent. He gave a very critical review of political events occurring recently, describing the European situation, etc. Retention was extremely good. Retained eight digits. Gave addresses correctly at the end of five minutes, as well as named objects shown. Calculation was unusually good. Could multiply three digits by three digits correctly. The seven from a hundred tests was performed quickly and accurately. Speech and writing were normal. Patient felt that he should have justice, that the courts of the city should help him, if not, he would go to Washington or take the law in his own hands, and defend himself against his persecutors.

PHYSICAL EXAMINATION. Patient was in excellent physical condition. Height 5′ 6″ and weight 150 pounds. All systems normal. Blood pressure 125/80. Laboratory reports including urine, blood chemistry, etc., were normal in every detail.

During the patient's stay in the hospital his mental status showed practically no change. He did not appear to have deteriorated further. He adhered to his delusions of persecution, but these delusions varied. At times they were directed against his wife and her relatives, later against various physicians, and again, against the Detective Bureau. He had absolutely no insight into his mental condition. He talked irrelevantly and incoherently on many occasions. He appeared to be always on his guard in his attitude toward ward patients and visiting relatives with whom he frequently refused to talk. He was committed one month after admission. Since that time he has deteriorated slowly.

The fourth case is an excellent example of a patient suffering from paranoid schizophrenia, who has been followed for several years. With the aid of modern treatment repeated with each flare-up in symptoms, she has had long periods of satisfactory adjustment, but with frequent exacerbations of her chronic symptoms.

Patient, a married white female, age 42, at the time of admission on August 8, 1938. According to the complaint, the patient had been accusing her son, her mother-in-law, and her friends, of attempting to poison her. She also believed that her husband had been unfaithful. According to the informant, an elder son, the patient has had great difficulty with her husband and has accused him to being unfaithful since shortly after their marriage 23 years prior to entry in the hospital. On several occasions she has been admitted to general hospitals for a few weeks rest for "nervous symptoms," consisting of temper outbursts directed toward the husband. During the period of her son's memory, these attacks have become increasingly severe, and accordingly during these attacks much of her conversation is incoherent and irrelevant. She has also expressed the fear that her money will be taken from her and that her home is to be sold. She has also felt that mariahuana fumes and ether are being used to poison her. The son states that she has always been inclined to read personal meanings into gestures and other actions of her friends and relatives. The developmental history reveals that the patient has been an interested active person, has played several musical instruments, had been a good student. Prior to her marriage, and occasionally since, she has worked either as a clerk in a drug store or in a music store. At one time she worked as a secretary in her husband's office. The son characterizes her as being talkative, pessimistic, and vain. The family history reveals a grandmother who committed suicide during a so-called menopausal psychosis, and another aunt who died in a large state hospital with some type of mental disorder, type unknown. On admission, the patient was extremely uncooperative and antagonistic toward the hospital staff. She was very suspicious, and expressed great anxiety concerning her presence in the hospital. Her speech was coherent but her answers to questions were always colored by her paranoid delusions. She tended to be overproductive except when she felt the person she was talking to was against her, then she would refuse to talk. She was having auditory and olfactory hallucinations. She was well oriented for time, place, and person. Memory was adequate. Clinical and laboratory examinations were performed in considerable detail and all proved to be within normal limits. Diagnosis was paranoid schizophrenia and insulin shock therapy was instituted. During the third week of insulin shock treatment, the patient began to show some improvement in her coöperation and expressed some insight concerning her delusions. Her attitude toward her son and husband improved remarkably, and while she still felt her husband had probably been unfaithful to her at times, she became much less antagonistic toward him. The son expressed the idea that his father probably has been unfaithful to the mother but he thought that his mother greatly exaggerated the extent and frequency of this.

At the time of discharge the patient was extremely meticulous of her appearance and we felt, at times, overly careful about being neatly and completely dressed and made-up. The etiologic factors were felt to be an unusually strict moral code drilled into the patient during her childhood and adolescence, she had an extremely poor attitude toward sexual matters and entered into marriage with no understanding of the physical factors involved in married life. Throughout her married life she was extremely frigid and had strong guilt feelings concerning marital relations. Because of this her husband apparently did not derive normal gratification from their marriage and apparently did resort to occasional periods of infidelity. Patient has been unable to emancipate herself from her mother, who is an extremely unstable and dictatorial person. She has also been unable to allow her children to emancipate and develop normally. These children are two very active boys who have attempted to break away from the home, and the beginning emancipation of the sons apparently precipitated the present attack. Following her discharge from the hospital, she was advised to continue follow-up treatment in the clinic. The date of discharge was November 5, 1938. Patient was seen on one or two occasions in clinic, but was not very faithful about keeping up her contact. She was next seen on May 27, 1939, at which time she returned to the hospital with the information that she had gotten along pretty well during the interval until about three weeks prior to readmission. During this past three weeks she had become more hyperactive, irritable, suspicious, and unreasonable. Her son feared she was having another attack and brought her to the hospital.

On readmission the patient was again quite paranoid, expressed many peculiar ideas and had many paranoid delusions. She also had some odd sensations about the pelvis which she finally expressed as being due to a fear that the contraceptive suppository she had been using might have injured her genital organs. She then stated that she had been having sexual relations with another man and was having considerable guilt feelings about this. During the interval, the patient's husband died but she states that she believes he is still alive and states she is inclined to believe in reincarnation. She frankly confessed to auditory hallucinations, stating she could hear her husband's voice. When asked if she had visual hallucinations, she became very angry, stating that that would be a sign of insanity. Physical examination again was entirely normal. Laboratory examinations are within normal limits. This patient was committed to a large state hospital on June 27, 1939 for further treatment and care. Patient remained in the state hospital until September 23, 1939, at which time she returned to her home in Denver on parole and stayed until December 1939, when she returned to the large state hospital and was finally released on June 23, 1940. In the interval between that and the time of her admission on December 16, 1942, the patient had gotten along fairly well. She had worked in various stores around town, had managed her small resources rather well, and had made an adequate adjustment in the community. She had been carrying on sexual relations with a married man in town with apparent satisfaction to herself, this being in sharp contrast to her behavior during marriage. Recently she had become rather upset over a business deal in which she lost a small sum of money. She felt that somehow the Germans and Catholics were mixed up in her loss of money. She was also quite distressed over her young son's presence in the Army and felt that he had committed some crime for which he was to be punished. During this admission the patient continued to show paranoid delusions, felt that she had been inoculated with syphilis and the doctor was treating her for syphilis unknown to her. She also felt that her elder son was against her and he and his wife were attempting to deprive her of all of her property. She had ideas of reference, but no hallucinations were elicited at this time. Clinical and laboratory examination were still entirely normal, although the patient has gained considerable weight since her last admission. Patient improved in a few days after admission and most of her symptoms disappeared except for the paranoid trends, and she was discharged without any special treatment. She was re-admitted on May 11, 1945 following a period in which she became confused and during which time she became neglectful of her person. She seemed unable to care for herself, and would do odd things, such as bringing the neighbor's washing into her own home, forgetting to buy food, and neglecting to send the laundry out.

Mental status examination revealed the presence of marked confusion and bewilderment. She talked slowly and with much hesitation. She had difficulty in expressing herself clearly. At times she would become rather agitated because of fears produced by her paranoid ideas. Because of the patient's deterioration and because her symptoms consisted merely in neglect of her person and some confusion, it was not felt necessary to give her further shock therapy and she was dismissed in the custody of her family with advice that they give her the equivalent of special attendant's care at home. She was dismissed and has not been seen since that time.

The fifth case is a good example of simple schizophrenia.

F. R. is a 29-year-old white male, brought to the clinic by his mother for an examination. She states that he is worried about himself, has no ambition, and cannot seem to decide what he wants to do. Mother states that the illness had its onset in infancy when he had colitis. This, she states, was caused by his being fed a pickle by one of the neighbor women. She states that since then he has had a variety of diagnoses being called hysteria, schizophrenia and so forth. She states she is not satisfied with any of these opinions and wants a new one. Mother states that following the pickle episode as a child, he was critically ill but recovered. His parents were separated while the patient was an infant and it has been necessary for the mother to work. As a result he has been cared for by servants. She states that at one time during his infancy they had a luetic maid. The family were all checked with Blood Wassermann and all found to be negative. She states that when he was 16 they again had a luetic servant, but they were all tested again and at this time, the patient had a 3+ Blood Wassermann. She states he was given three odd shots and had no further treatment. The patient told an uncle that he had contracted the infection while away on a merchant vessel as a sailor. Also during his early childhood the patient had an abscess which was thought to be a sarcoma but an operation was performed and the patient recovered. Mother also states that he had malaria during childhood. After recovering from the malaria, he had an accident and bumped his head. He states this made him feel nervous and a few weeks later he began to think he was losing his mind. He developed ideas that people were talking about him. One physician told him to go to New Orelans, and his mother took him to a local physician. She states he was placed on vitamin therapy, left the hospital and had a quarrel with one of the doctors and with the police department. He refused to stay in the hospital and returned home. Mother's reaction to his illness was that it wasn't serious. She and the patient obtained a book on the subject, read up on it, and following this she states he seemed to improve. He then took a course in flying and progressed to the point of soloing. He then entered the Army as a private, was promoted to corporal, and the mother interfered, and after talking to his commanding officer, the patient was made a flying cadet. He states he was unable to relax at this job, went A.W.O.L. and came home. He returned to the Army airfield and when they arrived for him, the patient had gone to get a haircut. He then returned to the psychiatric unit at the airfield and was dismissed. He then consulted another physician who gave him four electroshock treatments. These made the patient feel so good that he quit and went to Colorado on a fishing trip. He then volunteered for the American Field Service as an ambulance driver but was rejected on psychiatric basis. At this same time he began to drink heavily and while drinking on a fishing trip he was involved in an accident and almost drowned. Mother then placed him in the hands of a series of psychiatrists in rapid succession always withdrawing him from treatment in each instance. Patient finally committed himself as a voluntary patient to one of the state hospitals but after a spinal puncture was performed decided to leave. Throughout the examination the mother was hovering, overprotective, and oversolicitous to the patient's welfare. Physical status was thin but otherwise entirely normal. Patient was coöperative. Mental status examination revealed a rather tense and perplexed facies. When not talking he would frequently sigh deeply, groan, and touch himself. He thinks these symptoms are due to the fact that he is short of breath. There is great difficulty in formulating his words and expressing himself clearly. After explaining the origin of his pain he would go into a long, irrelevant, inconsequential story. Psychomotor activity was definitely reduced. He seemed rather indifferent to most of the events in the environment although he would participate in conversation if someone else took the initiative. At times he would become annoyed and irritable. This was most marked when his mother was present but was also seen at other times. There was no disturbance in sleeping or in eating habits. Patient had no hallucinations at the time of the original examination but had many somatic preoccupations which approached delusional proportions. He also complained of difficulty in thinking, stating "words become stuck in my head." He always indicated the right parietal region as the area in which the words became stuck. He states that in the past he has imagined he heard voices and had some ideas people were after him but these ideas were no longer present. The patient has some insight of a superficial sort and stated that he felt like someone who was standing on a hot stove. He believes that he will ultimately "blow up" and become uncontrollable.

It was felt that circumstances of a broken home, an oversolicitous mother and the effect of her concern over his condition had resulted in this state. Patient has been followed for approximately five years and during this time has continued to show little change in his course. Mother has continued to take him from one physician to another, seldom following the recommendations of any unless it happens to be her own concept of his condition. The patient has been institutionalized and is in a chronic schizoid state. The somatic preoccupations and delusions are essentially unchanged.

An occasional patient will be seen who shows a very acute malignant-appearing schizophrenic-like psychosis. Some of these patients will be mute with catatonic posturing and show all the signs of an acute schizophrenic stupor. Others will show an acute hallucinatory or paranoid reaction in the setting of a clear sensorium and look like an acute paranoid onset of schizophrenia. The factor that distinguishes these patients from the ordinary schizophrenic group is that they tend to clear up in a matter of two to seven days without anything special in the way of treatment. In some instances intravenous amytal and prolonged rest will bring about a very prompt recovery. These patients have been seen by the authors in two settings. The first group occurred in the days of the C.C. Camp, when youngsters from underprivileged homes were placed for the first time in a barracks life far away from home and often in isolated communities. Some of these youngsters, after receiving much good-natured kidding, often being the butt of the rather crude jokes of their fellow workers, would develop acute schizoid reactions. Because they cleared up promptly it was felt they were not properly diagnosed as schizophrenia and at the time the local term for them was "malignant homesickness." In all of these cases the patient cleared up with a single amytal interview and with assurance that he would be discharged to his home. During World War II, many malignant schizophrenic-like reactions were reported, most of them occurring in a setting of prolonged fatigue and in combat situations. They were frequently dubbed "three-day schizophrenia." Most of these cases recovered with amazing celerity. Sometimes the clinical picture was definitely catatonic but other schizophrenic manifestations, including paranoid reactions, were encountered. At first these patients were evacuated, only to have recovery occur en route in a few days. Apparently physical stress, long-continued emotional experiences may elicit a schizophrenic-like response even in a well-integrated personality.

Another type of reaction which is a part of the schizophrenic picture is the so-called "folie à deux" phenomenon. This is an old term used to describe cases in which one member of the family, either a sibling, parent, husband, or wife will develop a typical schizophrenic psychosis from one of the above varieties. A second member of the group may develop a psychosis simulating the schizophrenic psychosis but the psychosis in the second person is on a hysterical and imitative basis. At the onset some of these cases so closely simulate the original disorder that it is at times almost impossible to distinguish which one is truly psychotic and which one is showing the hysterical, imitative behavior. In fact, in some instances, both patients appear to have an identical psychosis but in most carefully followed reports it will be found that one responds very dramatically to therapy and the other tends to run the usual course of a serious schizophrenic episode.

Diagnosis. Perhaps the symptomatic markings have been made sufficiently clear so that the percentage of diagnostic accuracy should be fairly high. The chief differential diagnostic difficulty concerns manic-depressive psychosis. Theoretically, and on paper, the distinction is simple, but in actual practice it may for a long time be surprisingly difficult. In given cases, the diagnostic day is only saved by a careful review of the patient's life history in longitudinal section. Here one may utilize advantageously an evaluation of the prepsychotic personality. In the manic-depressive the predominance of social, extroverted and syntonic qualities and in the schizophrenic, the prominence of asocial, introverted, and schizoid traits.

From the vantage point of the psychosis itself, the best help is to be attained from a careful estimate of the affective state. If depression exists, it is in manic-depressive evidenced by a definite subjective feeling of sadness and, in general, is of such a type that the detached observer would from the physical and verbal expressions of the patient readily label it as melancholia. In schizophrenia, on the other hand, no strong subjective feeling can be detected and neither the motor expression movements of the patient nor the quality of his verbal explanations stamp the depression as genuine and of the type that is ordinarily experienced in miniature in normal mental life. In other words, there is in the schizophrenic, a discrepancy between his mood and his thoughts.

The excitement of the manic-depressive is in fairly close contact with the environment; there is in it a connectivity and sequence of thought producing so-called "flight of ideas"; whatever the prevailing mood may be, it is genuine as judged by the usual criteria and finally, it has a rather prolonged course. In schizophrenia, the catatonic and other excitements seemingly are not related to the environment nor do they derive stimulus from the surroundings. The thoughts expressed in the excitement seem like discrete islets not connected with each other and an analysis of the productions would indicate poverty rather than profusion of thought. The emotional expressions would have to be labelled inadequate and contradictory and the excitements are short lived and often appear and disappear many times in the course of the psychosis. Fairly frequently they represent emergences from stupors.

The student may be given some additional help from the appended table.

Table 10

MAIN DIFFERENTIAL DIAGNOSIS OF SCHIZOPHRENIA AND MANIC-DEPRESSIVE PSYCHOSES

Findings in Mental Examination	*Schizophrenia*	*Manic Reaction*	*Depressive Reaction*
1. General behavior and activity.	Odd, incongruous, silliness, irrelevance and incoherence of stream of thought.	Pressure of talk and activity. Flight of ideas and distractibility. Overproductivity.	Slowness of thought and activity. Depressed facies. Underproductivity.
2. Affective disorder present.	Loss of affect of inadequate affect.	A frank elation or quick oscillations.	A frank depression.
3. Trend reactions.	Delusions of various types, ideas of reference, ideas of influence, paranoid ideas. Hallucinations usually prominent.	Expansive ideas to fit in with elation. No hallucinations.	Self-condemnation and self-recrimination to fit in with depressive affect. Hallucinations rare.
4. Sensorium changes.	Sensorium generally clear. Insight usually absent.	Clear. Insight may be present.	Clear. Insight often present.

Prognosis. Scientific forecasting or prognosis is a sadly neglected aspect of psychiatry. Too often it is only an echo of diagnosis. If this is so in schizophrenia much that is important and, perhaps, particularly, valuable sources of information and needed treatment concepts will be lost. An opinion as to outcome is only permissible after a thorough review, not only of the psychosis itself, but of the whole life history of the individual, an extremely careful weighing of the potential assets of the patient and an estimate of the chances of recasting his environment. It is very difficult to arrive at any satisfactory conclusions concerning the recovery rate and by various authors it is placed from zero to such fancifully high figures as 80 per cent. In the latter, it is obvious that many reactions that are not really schizophrenic have been included. The criteria of recovery occasions further difficulty since the schizophrenic process may be arrested at various levels below the complete recovery level, descending from partial social readjustments to mere cessation of certain symptoms permitting life in the home instead of in a mental hospital. The various psychoanalytic schools measure the malignancy by the depth of the regression of the patient to infantile and intrauterine and even phylogenetically primitive stages of evolution. Catatonia is commonly believed to be more favorable in outcome than the other types.

One of us made an intensive study of a group of patients who unquestionably recovered from schizophrenia. The recoveries have all endured more than five years and no psychotic episodes that might suggest an original manic-depressive instead of a schizophrenia have appeared. The recovery rate was somewhat higher in the Russian Jews.

It is important to differentiate between what might be termed a constitutional "shut-in" type and one which is wholly or in part the product of environment. The former develops in spite of normal or at least average surroundings; the latter is a feasible defense against definitely inimical reality. Other things being equal, the first argues for an unfavorable prognosis; the second does not necessarily weigh against recovery. Such a differentiation was possible in two of the patients:

The first patient was markedly seclusive in her own family circle, but on analysis this seclusiveness resolved itself into a not illogical tendency to escape hopeless conditions. Towards those who stood outside the family circle, and particularly those who had superior educational assets, she was not seclusive. On the contrary she was demonstrative and formed passionate attachments for them. Presumably the patient was the highest product of a very diseased family stock and from childhood sought to raise herself above its low and sordid plane. The personal weapons which were unconsciously forged to accomplish this purpose were ambition, a love of the dramatic, and a childlike imitation of those who were admired. Thus, all in all, the personality, particularly the seclusiveness, was a logical defense against an inimical environment. During the psychosis, which was quite schizophrenic, there was the persistent wish to cut herself off from her family.

In the second patient there was likewise seclusiveness, and again it was clearly a refuge from the hard facts of the patient's life. The patient, at 17 years of age, lived on a remote farm; existence was rigid and monotonous, actual necessities were denied and there was that type of stern religion which regards beauty as sinful. Even the mode of dress was prescribed, and a drab and shapeless garb had to be worn. Defective socialization reached a high degree and during a rather typical schizophrenic psychosis this withdrawal was pronounced. An excellent recovery was obtained, however. The prepsychotic mental isolation should have been regarded as a logical reaction, the only available protection against an unnatural environment. In one sense the patient's withdrawal was an effort, not so much to seek relief in unreality as to hold on to the worthwhile things of reality.

In three patients who recovered from what seemed to be clear-cut catatonic schizophrenic reactions, there was a dispositional character best described as stubbornness. It included a marked opposition to the acceptance of contrary opinions and undesirable situations. In one, a physical reaction pattern had become ingrained and "even as a child she would stiffen herself, open her mouth and roll her eyes about if opposed in any way." In another it was the result of a spoiling process in an only child and anger appeared from "the slightest opposition or interference." The third, in childhood, was "markedly stubborn" and "hard to conquer." It is noteworthy that each of these individuals when confronted with concrete difficulties (illegitimate pregnancies in two instances and a serious conflict with the authority of a school board in the third) became psychotic and furthermore manifested blind catatonic outbreaks against this environment. That this "catatonia" may have been merely the pathologic accentuation of prepsychotic "make-up" is worth consideration in prognosis.

In three patients, the personality contained a tendency toward mysticism. In the first, an unusually long retention of the "pretend stage" of childhood developed, in the early teens, into a concentrated interest in Hindu occultism. The second was a firm believer in telepathy, and the third was grossly superstitious and readily influenced. In the psychoses which occurred, the somewhat vague paranoid delusional formation was of the kind which seems to draw its substance from a background of unreality. More favorable prognosis is implied in the supposition that the precox-like symptoms were merely the outgrowth of personal habits of belief and not due to a disintegration of self.

In three patients prepsychotic sensitiveness and paranoid tendencies had existed. These were increased by complicating conditions, and in one case an unsatisfactory marriage sharpened the distrust. The psychoses were all paranoid with much to indicate splitting. There were complete recoveries, however. The important prognostic point is that after all no deterioration of personality was involved.

The percentage of precipitating situations that could be fairly regarded as serious and significant was high in the group of recovered patients.

We believe that an abrupt, stormy onset is a relatively favorable prognostic sign and probably represents the struggle of the personality against the acceptance of the psychotic material. This view is concurred in by Barrett, Sullivan and others. At the onset, too, inhibition is enormously diminished and the patient is very susceptible to outside influences, which may, from time to time later in the psychosis, impart a false appearance of malignancy. Thus, in a woman 36 years old, who made an excellent recovery, the reading of lurid detective stories at the onset imparted a strong paranoid trend to the psychosis and determined a very bizarre expression; "violet ray," "poisoned food," "throwing gas," "dictaphones," "germs," "poisoned daggers shot into the brain," etc.

Finally, it is prognostically helpful to view the patient from the standpoint of his environment and to attempt to form some judgment as to the chances of obtaining a fairly adequate satisfaction from reality. In schizophrenia there are only two stages. First, the stage of conflict which is essentially the struggle against submergence by unreality. Then, if recovery does not occur, there is, second, the final state of pathologic adjustment or unreality. Clinically it is deterioration. Sometime during the conflict, it is reasonable to assume that the chances offered by reality are unconsciously weighted against the surcease of the nirvana of unreality. The question arises as to how far these promises are to be realized and to what degree the psychotic hopes which held back chronicity were fulfilled. It is possible to deal only with the fairly obvious, which must be a very small fraction of the entire picture.

Otto Kant, in reviewing the prognostic criteria in schizophrenia, noted that a persistence of uniform behavior and psychotic symptomatology was a benign sign. Lack of uniformity in behavior and symptomatology was considered a malignant sign only if it occurred in the setting of clear consciousness. A favorable sign was the presence of primary changes in the emotional sphere of either a manic or depressive state. The presence of psychogenic factors in the precipitation of the case were of good prognostic value if environmentally induced but bad if these factors were due to the patient's own attitude.

Treatment: PROPHYLAXIS. Schizophrenia, once it begins, becomes all too early and all too soon a fixed and chronic psychotic maladaptation and it is therefore highly important that the prophylactic opportunities be intensively cultivated. Such opportunities occur strikingly during childhood, and less emphatically but still definitely enough in early adult life. So far, no satisfactory pharmacologic, endocrine, or other physical approach has been derived from pathology, and the better chance is to be found in the possibilities of modifying the personality, variously described as "introverted," "seclusive," "schizoid," etc., upon which schizophrenia is so readily engrafted. The prophylactic objective should be to strive for a more even balance between individual and environment and in some degree "exteriorize" or socialize him.

For the child, the home should be first and foremost a place in which it may find an atmosphere of harmony and happiness. There should be neither unduly harsh discipline nor its opposite, spoiling. Competition between brothers and sisters, in the home for the favor of the parents, particularly when spurred on by "playing favorites" by the parents is pernicious. The attempt to stimulate a child by too constantly pointing out the assets in brothers or sisters usually results in the production of inferiority feelings and is a hazardous process. There should be liberal doses of explanation to the child in the parent-child relationship and particularly should punishment contain a generous leaven of explanation. Companionship with other children of both sexes, outdoors, athletics, and all reasonable socializing influences should be encouraged. It should be made easy for the child to bring his playmates into the home and there should be no risk that things would be seen or heard there that would shame him before other children. Sex and particularly the concrete facts of sex are always difficult for the potential schizophrenic and "therefore effort should be made to prevent phantasy by supplying competent knowledge of sex hygiene, and to discourage rumination by always discussing such matters without emotion and with only a modicum of moralization." Sex instruction should be begun comparatively early in childhood but, naturally in a degree and in detail suitable to the age of the child.

Children have toward their parents an attitude of idealistic-identification. Unconsciously, they supplement their own weakness by identifying themselves in the parents. Here is a strong emotional bond, leading to indiscriminate imitation and containing sources of danger, particularly for the introverted child. The goal of any real psychology of childhood is to obtain for the child a true psychologic maturity. If this is not accomplished, the child is destined for a life of slavish imitation of those who become the emotional surrogates for his parents. The parent-child bond must be loosened not too abruptly but nevertheless, surely, and independence of thought and action must be wisely and continuously encouraged.

Introverted children read a great deal and while their reading should not be too rigidly ordered, yet it should be directed toward types of literature that are not too luridly and completely phantastic. Religion supplies an important need and it should be a source of beauty and inspiration but social and practical too, and above all not grimly fear producing. According to Hamilton:

> The schooling of these children should be carefully scanned and means found to check the tendency to study abstruse and obscure subjects. Rather should socializing subjects be emphasized, that youth may keep close to facts and maintain friendly personal contacts. Primacy in competition of intellects is a goal to be disparaged . . . the choice and any change of occupation should be given consideration by those interested in order to prevent the development of illness; and any inclination to choose a vocation that merely promises compensation for ill-recognized inferiority feelings should be skillfully handled. The vocation selected should be certainly within the capacity of the individual and of a type to maintain his social life on as broad a scale as may be within his power.

These are but a few of the conceptions that may be advantageously utilized in the attempt to prevent the development of schizophrenia not only

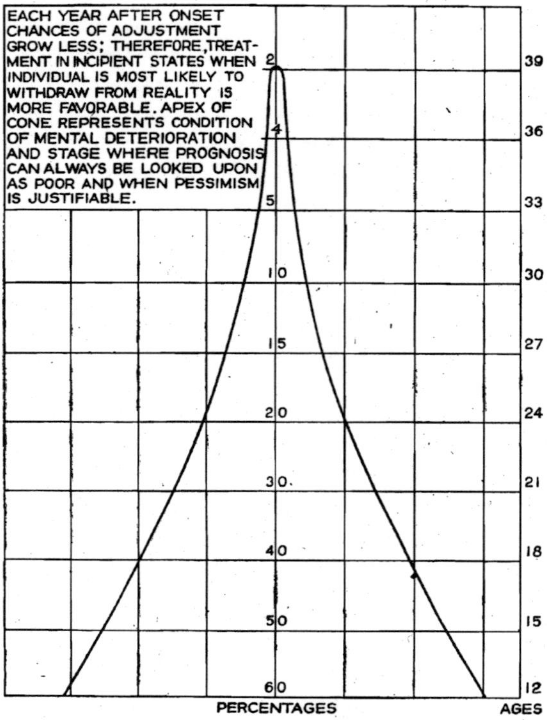

FIG. 25.

in children but even later in life in those ingrowing personalities who are in danger of this chronic maladjustment.

Treatment of the Psychosis. Obviously the earlier the actual schizophrenia is treated correctly, the better the chance of adjustment. The accompanying chart graphically illustrates this point.

In combating schizophrenia the psychiatrist needs the inspiration of a workable conception. We know of no better conception than the psychobiologic interpretation of Meyer. It views the patient critically in the long section of his life history and particularly surveys the series of maladaptations that preceded the final schizophrenic one. It then asks such pertinent and therapeutically stimulating questions as these: What are the resources of the patient? What has he to react with? What is the situation he is called on to meet? Can we modify his resources in order to enable him better to meet the situation, or can we modify the situation so he may better meet it with his resources? Etc. Finally, the psychobiologic idea does not court exclusively any single therapeutic mistress and it leaves open the door of every reasonable treatment plan.

PSYCHOTHERAPY. There are many kinds of psychotherapy and, we believe the more individualistic the approach the better. Generally speaking the psychiatrist will find his patient living on the plane of unreality or dangerously close to it. Between this and the reality which is possible for the patient and which varies for each patient there is a gulf which must be bridged if adjustment is to be secured. The steps between phantasy and reality cannot be forced too abruptly but must be taken, psychologically speaking, slowly and gradually. The building up of confidence, persuasion, suggestion, particularly the indirect suggestion that skillfully and not too obviously puts forth the claims of reality, are helpful. All this implies some degree of accessibility on the part of the patient but, so is this a requisite for any form of psychotherapy and in the bulk of early cases some degree of accessibility is at hand. Once a bit of insight is secured and there is some beginning of the process of viewing the symptoms objectively, then this advantage should be pressed and expanded.

There is much difference of opinion concerning that specialized form of psychotherapy known as psychoanalysis. Some authorities feel that dangerous panics result from the inability of the patient to face the probably incestuous significance of the phantasies, and that the physician becomes a part of the phantasy. Others think that this is merely a difficult place in the treatment plan and that it can be won through. It is obvious that in any event psychoanalysis must be modified if it is to be used in the treatment of the schizophrenic.

From the standpoint of formal psychoanalysis, Zilboorg writes:

> The psychoanalytical method, as is known, requires a strictly passive attitude on the part of the investigator, interpretations and explanations being given to the patient only when the patient is affectively ready, i.e., when the patient through the accumulation or display of the affect which is related to this or that trend, is about ready to gain insight almost entirely without explanations or interpretations. This method, if properly applied, thus excludes any intellectualization—the chief enemy of insight, and in schizophrenia the most dangerous enemy, because the schizophrenic is an intellectualist par excellence; he could, would and does indulge in most complex intellectual formulations in order to avoid the necessity of emotional participation in reality. Another advantage derived from the psychoanalytical method is that if a patient is permitted to talk and "ramble along" freely without interference, he sooner or later, but quite invariably stumbles upon "resistances," i.e., upon psychological elements which are charged with a great deal of affect. It is possible to observe quite clearly and even to estimate the depth of the affect long before it comes to full expression. The patient's voice, minor and major gesticulations, facies, sudden silences, evasions, all serve as excellent indicators and signs of warning.
>
> The method is called "affective re-integration" . . . One fact, however, appears beyond doubt. The analytical method in its classical form, preceded by a preliminary and rather long period of analysis of the "reality principle," mobilizes the masses of affective energies which otherwise remain shut-in and prevent a proper contact with reality.
>
> The significance of this cannot be overlooked. It throws a somewhat different light on the phenomenon of Schizoidie. It is not impossible that what is called schizoid personality is actually not an established constitutional form, but a complex resultant, a derivative of certain dispositions only. Under circumstances of

great stress, such as an unusually strict, repressive, parental ideal, combined with very early traumatic stimulations of sexual life, a conflict ensues which favors the withdrawal of the affect from active contact with reality—and thus occurs the overemphasis of the schizoid disposition.

The affect can be mobilized and set to expression. If the mobilization takes place after reality and phantasy have been differentiated by the patient, the process of affective re-integration may go to its completion.

Irrespective of the therapeutic value of "affective reintegration" it is obvious that in its present form it can scarcely have any extensive application, since in the treatment of one patient, there were 450 one hour interviews. If it has any value at all it would be from the angle of psychopathologic research.

Drug Therapy. Naturally in the treatment of schizophrenia, in which the patient may be mentally sick for many years and often for the remainder of his life span, the need for drug therapy of various kinds to treat intercurrent conditions will arise. In the psychosis itself, the appearance of excitements, insomnia, etc., may call for the use of sedatives. There is a wide range of selection, veronal, paraldehyde, hyoscine, the barbituric acid group particularly sodium amytal, etc. Sodium amytal has been utilized in the production of narcosis, especially in catatonia, in doses of 0.6 to 1.0 gr. intravenously, often along with oral, intramuscular, and rectal administration. Lorenz states one of the theories as follows:

That an individual develops a psychosis following normal mental life. Assuming that this psychosis in the case of katatonia is at a much lower level of mental existence than the normal, and may even be a subjugation to the more primitive fetal existence—yet it is not as deep as real unconsciousness. If at this point one precipitates a katatonic patient into unconsciousness by the use of a narcotic or anesthetic agent one pierces through this level of katatonic stupor and dislodges the katatonic mechanism.

Upon the return from unconsciousness induced by drug the katatonic patient mentally approaches the so-called normal. After he has regained this normal mental life, the various factors and stimuli responsible for his original psychosis become effective; and after a period of hours he reverts back to this more primitive level which is apparently a more desirable refuge.

Nevertheless, I have repeatedly observed considerable improvement and in one instance, at least, a satisfactory adjustment following the induction of rather prolonged narcosis by my assistant, Dr. Harold Palmer. Lundvall, Donath and Kieholz report good results with sodium nucleinate, Ishida and Holmes with sodium chloride infusions, Ludlum and Corson-White with endocrine preparations. Various investigators have reported failures with endocrine preparations, with somniferin, with trional, with cocaine hydrochloride, and with the metallic salts. Surgical procedures do not offer very much. The enthusiastic reports of Cotton as to the benefits accruing from the removal of focal infection in teeth, tonsils, sinuses, prostate, female pelvis, intestinal tract, etc., have not been substantiated. It is, however, good medical and psychiatric judgment to clear up when it is feasible such *real* focal infection as is present. The results of the surgical induction of an aseptic meningitis have been disappointing. Attention to the gastrointestinal tract from the standpoint of its proper functioning and the reduction of the number of putrefactive organisms by the employment of b. Acidophilus milk should be followed. In general, all proper hygiene measures, psychotherapy, hydrotherapy, pyrotherapy, exercise, etc. are indicated in the intelligent treatment of schizophrenic patients.

INSULIN SHOCK. Pharmacologic shock therapy in some form is used in the majority of hospitals caring for schizophrenic patients. The most satisfactory results from the standpoint of well-sustained improvement is obtained with insulin or hypoglycemic shock as suggested by Sakel. In our hands the results have been essentially the same as those of Ross and his co-workers whose statistics are here presented in part.

Table 11

CONDITION OF PATIENTS WITH DEMENTIA PRECOX AT THE TERMINATION OF TREATMENT, IN PER CENT, ACCORDING TO THE TYPE OF TREATMENT

	Totals	*Recovered*	*Much Improved*	*Improved*	*Unimproved*	*Died*
Insulin	100.0	11.1	26.5	26.0	35.2	1.1
Metrazol	100.0	1.6	9.9	24.5	63.5	0.5
Control group	100.0	3.5	11.2	7.4	73.3	4.6

In our experience the method is of greatest value in rendering uncoöperative, delusional patients accessible for detailed psychotherapeutic procedures. In many instances patients who are mute, preoccupied, or antagonistic become coöperative, participate in ward activities and become interested in reaching an understanding of their reaction and in forming adequate plans for the future. The technique of insulin shock therapy should be thoroughly mastered in some institution using this type of treatment before it is undertaken.

The treatment is arduous and dangerous in unskilled hands. It is not suited to office or home administration and should be given only in well-equipped, modern hospitals. The treatment should be administered by a central insulin service or department within the hospital. The patients should have a complete physical check including such laboratory procedures as electrocardiogram, chest x-ray and complete blood chemistry studies. Persons showing evidence of metabolic disturbance, pulmonary infection or myocardial damage should be rejected for this form of therapy. In addition to the careful routine history and mental status examination the Rorschach test, association motor studies, and certain of the thinking disorder tests are indicated. All of these examinations should be repeated during the course of the treatment and following its completion as they offer much information as to the nature and quality of the remission obtained. Harris and Horowitz have used a pre-insulin sodium amytal interview and find it of prognostic value, thus making for a better selection of patients for the insulin group. We have not used it in just this manner, but find the method of value in getting detailed examinations upon patients who fail to coöperate to detailed testing in the pretreatment period.

The administration of the shock itself is relatively simple in trained hands.

1. Treatments are administered daily excepting one rest day each week. On this day insulin units 15 is routinely given.

2. The evenings before treatment patients are given a light supper at 5:30 P.M. and no food until after the shock period the following day.

3. "Old" or ordinary insulin is given with an initial intramuscular dose of 15 units. The dose is increased 10 to 20 units per day until the patient reaches the stage of somnolence, profuse perspiration or muscular twitchings. The dosage is then increased only 5 units daily until the deep shock phase is attained. Protamin zinc insulin is unsatisfactory for these treatments.

4. In the deep shock phase the dosage remains constant unless the clinical course of the shock indicates an increase or decrease in the dosage.

The depth of shock bears little relation to the dosage of insulin in a series of cases, persons showing varying degrees of sensitivity to the medication.

In any individual case the depth of shock is roughly proportional to the insulin dose, but the total dose, as stated above, varies greatly from one person to another.

The depth of shock can be judged and controlled only by the clinical findings. The signs of shock are as follows:

1. PRESHOCK PHASE. Patient somnolent. Can be aroused. In later stage of this phase may show sweating or mild myoclonic twitchings. In the early phases of this stage, patients tend to rouse spontaneously after 30 to 60 minutes of somnolence. They may be rather confused. Termination by allowing patient to drink 50 per cent sugar solution until he ingests 2 Gm. of sugar per unit of insulin dosage.

2. SHOCK PHASE. In this phase the majority of patients show "wet shock." Perspiration is profuse, pulse rapid and thready, temperature drops, heart sounds mushy, blood pressure 80 to 90 over 60 to 70, skin pale, wet and cold, respirations deep and stertorous. There is usually profuse salivation with drooling, and patients should be restrained in a sitting position with neck flexed slightly forward to prevent aspiration of the saliva. In this stage patients are in deep coma, the tendon reflexes are hyperactive, ankle and patellar clonus are present, corneal reflex abolished, cough reflex usually absent and pathologic toe and thumb signs are elicited. After approximately 1 to 2½ hours the perspiration decreases and the skin becomes dry. The usual time of termination is after 1 hour of shock. The patient is given 2 Gm. of sugar per unit of insulin dosage as a 50 per cent sugar solution administered by means of a stomach tube inserted through the nose, or in some instances,

50 cc. of 50 per cent glucose I.V. Certain patients fail to perspire and are said to be in "dry shock." The signs are essentially the same as those listed above excepting the perspiration, and the salivation is often less marked. In this type of reaction many persons show myoclonic twitchings and in some instances a typical tonic-clonic convulsion. It is our practice to terminate the particular shock session after a convulsion, but the series of treatments is continued uninterrupted. In our experience patients have fewer complications if fluids and sodium chloride are forced between treatments to replace the loss through perspiration during the shock phase. It is believed that this shock phase is essential for therapeutic results.

3. COMPLICATIONS. Complications are infrequent in properly conducted departments. Convulsions may occur in any shock case at any time. They are usually self-limited and the shock may be terminated by the usual method after they subside. If they persist the treatment should be terminated by intravenous glucose in 50 per cent solution. Cardiac or respiratory collapse may occur but are infrequent. Administration of 50 per cent glucose I.V., epinephrin 3 to 6 minimums I.V. and oxygen inhalations usually restore these functions in short order. The most serious complication is prolonged or persistent coma. If patients fail to respond within 30 minutes after the nasal gavage they should receive intravenous glucose in 50 per cent solution. If this fails to bring about a prompt reaction it is our practice to institute venoclysis of 1,000 cc. of 10 per cent glucose in Ringer's solution. If the patient shows any tendency to hyperpyrexia 1,000 cc of whole blood as a transfusion is also administered. Continued coma or any signs of muscular twitchings are indicated for spinal drainage. To date such treatment has brought about a response within 1 to 12 hours in our experience, but deaths have been reported from this complication.

Complications such as aspiration pneumonia, pulmonary edema are usually avoided by careful nursing care during the shock phase.

The shock treatment is usually continued 30 to 50 days depending on the clinical progress of the patient. Daily progress notes by both physician and nurse are indispensable in the management of these individuals.

Termination of the series is by reduction of the insulin dosage over a period of 2 to 3 days.

An important phase of the treatment of these patients is an energetic regime of occupational therapy, ward responsibility, hydrotherapy, and daily therapeutic interviews as outlined elsewhere.

As previously stated, in our experience insulin serves only as a means of rendering a patient amenable to psychotherapy and if this important phase is omitted, relapse occurs in a disappointingly large number of cases.

Further details of the technique are described in the literature, but this information should, in all instances, be supplemented by practical experience with the method.

Metrazol, picrotoxin, nitrogen inhalations, coriamyrtin and other convulsant drugs have also been used as agents for pharmacologic shock. In the schizophrenias the results from the convulsant methods are of less benefit than in the affective disorders.

In spite of the numerous theories advanced to explain the benefits derived from shock therapy the treatment remains on an empirical basis.

General Management. In well-established schizophrenia the majority of the patients must be treated in suitable mental hospitals or sanitoria. In this way the medical interests of the patient, his safety, the safety of the community and the welfare and efficiency of the family are best protected and conserved. Under skillful supervision and, if satisfactory conditions are available, a number of patients may be cared for in the home, particularly during the "quiet" periods of the psychosis. In some instances farm or ranch life is a good solution. In early or mild cases, the Out-Patient Clinic or private physician can satisfactorily direct the care of the patient in the home. The placement of the patient in suitable homes and the community plan as it is followed at Gheel, Belgium, deserves wider recognition. Whether the patient be in hospital or at home, adequate nursing, occupational therapy and proper social service are important. The nurse is the representative of the psychiatrist and, if well trained, she will know how to attempt to check the inroads of phantasy and how to set forth in theory and practice the claims and advantages of reality. The social service worker if not too fanciful is especially valuable in the "follow-up" of adjusted patients and in the instance where patients are kept in the home, she should combat the danger of family disorganization. Occupational therapy is an extremely valuable and a necessary treatment adjunct. It is constantly symbolic of reality rather attractively garbed, and it produces the concrete fruits of work.

Treatment of Special Symptoms. The good nurse will know how necessary it is to see that the patient has sufficient nourishment; that he is tube fed when necessary; that he is kept clean, bathed frequently, changed when he wets or soils himself; that dangerous and sharp objects with which the patient might mutilate himself or others are not available; that the patient has enough exercise, sunshine and fresh air; that the chronic patient is taught useful habits and some routine, at least, in the care of the bodily functions and, the nurse, too, will minimize and control the physical dilapidation of appearance which is such an early result of the shutting out of reality. The prolonged bath, wet packs, etc., sometimes quiet the excited states. Apathy must be often the target of special measures: walks, calisthenics, physical culture apparatus, athletic games, indoor games, cards, other diversions, suitable motion pictures, and the theater, music, dancing, garden work, arts and crafts especially basketry and weaving, etc., are all helpful. Sometimes in stupor visiting by relatives is beneficial.

Total Push Therapy. Myerson and his co-workers have succeeded in instituting an intensive generalized therapeutic regime utilizing physiotherapy in its various forms, ultraviolet irradiation, careful attention to diet and vitamin intake, and an active program of exercise and games. Patients are attractively clothed and groomed. Coöperation in the plan is rewarded with extra privileges and infraction of the rule or lack of interest in the program results in the removal of certain privileges. They report a lowered incidence of chronic deteriorating processes, fewer instances of disturbed episodes and an increased incidence of discharges. The authors do not offer the plan as a cure for schizophrenia but show abundant evidence that the chronic schizophrenic can be taught to live more efficiently and pleasantly with his illness. The authors have utilized a program approximating this and find it of decided therapeutic benefit.

BIBLIOGRAPHY

Alzheimer: Beiträge zur Kenntnis der pathologischen Neuroglia und ihrer Beziehungen zu den Abbauvorgängen und Nervengeweibe, *Histol. u. histopath. Arbeiten, ü. d. Grosshirnrinde*, **3:** 401–562, 1910.

Arieti, S.: An interpretation of the divergent outcome of schizophrenia in identical twins, *Psychiatric Quart.*, **18:** 587, Oct., 1944.

Association for Research in Nervous and Mental Disease: "Schizophrenia (Dementia Praecox)," Vol. 5, 1925; "Schizophrenia," 1928 (see especially articles by Meyer, Brill, Pollock, Barrett, Myerson, Raphael, Sullivan, Hutchins, Whitehorn, Bowman, Henry, Lyz, White, Lewis, Dunlap, Freeman, Strecker, Hamilton); "Schizophrenia: An Investigation of the Most Recent Advances," 1931 (see especially articles by Malamud, Trentzch, Spielmeyer, Sullivan, Strecker, Zilboorg, Hensil, Bleckwenn), Baltimore, The Williams and Wilkins Co.

Bleuler, E.: "The Theory of Schizophrenic Negativism," Nervous and Mental Disease Monograph Series No. 11. New York, Nervous and Mental Disease Publishing Co.

Bowman, K. M., and G. P. Grabfield: Basal metabolism in mental disease, *Arch. Neurol. & Psychiat.*, **9:** 358–361, March, 1923.

———, J. Wortis, H. Fingert, and Julia Kogan: Results to date with pharmacological shock treatment of schizophrenia, *Am. J. Psychiat.*, **95:** 787, Jan., 1939.

Cameron, D. Ewen: "Objective and Experimental Psychiatry," 3rd ed., New York, The Macmillan Company, 1940.

Campbell, C. M.: A Modern conception of dementia praecox with five illustrative cases, *Rev. Neurol. & Psychiat.*, Edinburgh, **7:** 623–642, 1909; "The Treatment of Dementia Praecox and Allied Conditions," Modern Treatment Nervous and Mental Diseases, **1:** 590–613, 1913.

Corwin, William, and John W. Thompson: Treatment of the total organism in schizophrenic patients, *Am. J. Psychiat.*, **95:** 1059, March, 1939.

Cotton, H. A.: Fatty degeneration of the cerebral cortex in the psychoses with special reference to dementia praecox, *J. Exper. Med.*, **22:** 442, Oct., 1915.

Dunlap, C. B.: Dementia praecox—some preliminary observations on brains from carefully selected cases, and a consideration of certain sources of error, *Am. J. Psychiat.*, **3:** 403, Jan., 1924.

Freeman, Walter: "Deficiency of Catalytic Iron in the Brain in Schizophrenia: Schizophrenia, Association for Research in Nervous and Mental Diseases," **10:** 16, Baltimore, The Williams and Wilkins Company, 1931.

Frostig, J. P.: Sakel's pharmacologic shock treatment for schizophrenia: tentative directions and system of recording, (Translated by Joseph Wortis), *Arch. Neurol. and Psychiat.*, **39:** 219, Feb., 1938.

Funfgeld, E.: Ueber anatomische Untersuchungen bei Dementia praecox mit besonderer Berückisichtigung des Thalmus opticus, *Ztschr. f. d. ges. Neurol. u. Psychiat.*, **95:** 411–463, 1925.

Gellhorn, Ernst: The action of hypoglycemia on the central nervous system and the problem of schizophrenia from the physiologic point of view, *J.A.M.A.*, **110:** 1433, Apr. 30, 1938.

Gibbs, C. E.: Sex development and behavior in male patients with dementia praecox, *Arch. Neurol. & Psychiat.*, **9:** 73, Jan., 1923.

——: Sex development and behavior in female patients with dementia praecox, *Ibid.*, **11:** 179–194, Feb., 1924.

Greenacre, Phyllis: The content of the schizophrenic characteristics occurring in affective disorders, *Am. J. Insanity*, **75:** 197, Oct., 1918.

Harris, Meyer: Insulin sensitivity of patients with mental disease, *Arch. Neurol. & Psychiat.*, **48:** 761, 1942.

Harris, M. M., William A. Horwitz, and E. A. Milch: Regarding sodium amytal as a prognostic aid in insulin and metrazol shock therapy of mental patients (dementia praecox), *Am. J. Psychiat.*, **96:** 327, Sept., 1939.

Hemphill, R. E.: The significance of atrophy of the testis in schizophrenia, *J. Ment. Sc.*, **90:** 696, July, 1944.

———, M. Reiss, and A. L. Taylor: A study of the histology of the testis in schizophrenia and other mental disorders, *Ibid.*, **90:** 681, July, 1944.

Henderson, D. K., and R. D. Gillespie: "Text-Book of Psychiatry," Oxford University Press, 6th ed., 1944.

Hoch, August: Constitutional factors in the dementia praecox group, *Rev. Neurol. & Psychiat.*, **8:** 463–474, Aug., 1910.

Hoskins, R. G., and F. H. Sleeper: Endocrine factors in dementia praecox, *New England J. M.*, **200:** 361–369, Feb. 21, 1929.

———, and ———: Basal metabolism in schizophrenia, *Arch. Neurol. & Psychiat.*, **21:** 887–900, Apr., 1929.

———, and ———: Endocrine studies in dementia praecox, *Endocrinology*, **13:** 245–262, May–June, 1929.

———, and ———: A case of hebephrenic dementia praecox with marked improvement under thyroid treatment, *Endocrinology*, **13:** 459–466, Sept.–Oct., 1929.

Hunt, Robert C., Harold Feldman, and Rollin Fiero: Spontaneous remissions in dementia praecox, *Psychiatric Quart.*, **12:** 414, July, 1938.

Jelliffe, S. E.: The signs of pre-dementia praecox: their significance and pedagogic prophylaxis, *Am. J. M. Sc.* **134:** 157, 1907.

———: Dementia praecox and the vegetative nervous system, *New York M. J.*, **105:** 968, May, 1926.

Jung, C. G.: "The Psychology of Dementia Praecox," Nervous and Mental Disease Monograph Series No. 3, translated by A. A. Brill. New York, Nervous and Mental Disease Publishing Co.

Kant, Otto: The evaluation of prognostic criteria in schizophrenia, *J. Nerv. & Ment. Dis.*, **100:** 598, Dec., 1944.

Kasanin, J.: Blood sugar in schizophrenia, *Arch. Neurol. & Psychiat.*, **16:** 414, Oct., 1926.

———, and Eugenia Hanfmann: An experimental study of concept formation in schizophrenia, *Am. J. Psychiat.*, **95:** 35, July, 1938.

Katzenelbogen, S., Morris W. Brody, M. Hagman, and Ellis Margolin: Metrazol convulsions in men, *Ibid.*, **95:** 1343, May, 1939.

Kelly, O. F.: Acidophil degeneration in dementia praecox, *Ibid.*, **3:** 721–738, Apr., 1924.

Kitaboyashi, S.: *Mitt. a. d. med. Fak. d. kais. Kyushu Univ.*, 1924–1925.

Langfeldt, G.: Sympathetic system, with special regard to dementia praecox, *Norsk. mag. f. Lægevidensk.*, **86:** 1–32, Jan., 1925.

Lester, David: A study of prolonged coma following insulin shock, *Am. J. Psychiat.*, **95:** 1083, March, 1939.

Lewis, Nolan D. C.: "Constitutional Factors in Dementia Praecox," Monograph No. 35, Washington, D. C., Nervous & Mental Disease Publishing Co., 1923.

———, and Franz J. Kallmann: Personal communication on heredity in schizophrenia. To be published.

Lorenz, W. F.: Sugar tolerance in dementia praecox and other mental disorders, *Arch. Neurol. & Psychiat.*, **8:** 184, Aug., 1922.

Ludlum, S. D.: A study of the internal stigmas of degeneration in relation to metabolism and disturbance of the cerebral cortex in children, *Ibid.*, **7:** 167–173, Feb., 1922.

———: Physiologic conditions under which insanity occurs, **11:** 282, March, 1924.

Lugaro, Ernesto: "Modern Problems in Psychiatry," translated by David Orr and R. G. Rows, Manchester, University Press, 1909.

McFarland, R. A., and H. Goldstein: Biochemistry of dementia praecox, *Am. J. Psychiat.*, **94:** 509, Nov., 1938.

Malamud, William, and D. Rothchild: The Barrier Between the Blood and the Cerebrospinal Fluid, "The Distribution Ration of Bromides in Schizophrenia," Association for Research in Nervous and Mental Disease, **10:** 1–15, Baltimore, The Williams and Wilkins Company, 1931.

Malzberg, Benjamin: Outcome of insulin treatment in 1,000 patients with dementia praecox, *Psychiatric Quart.* **12:** 528, July, 1938.

———: A follow up study of patients with dementia praecox treated with insulin in the N. Y. Civil State Hospital, *Ment. Hyg.*, **23:** 641, July, 1939.

Marcuse, H.: *Obersteiners Arb.* Vol. 26.

Meduna, L. J.: Common factors in shock therapies, *Dis. Nerv. System*, **6:** 283, 1945.

Meyer, Adolf: Fundamental conceptions of dementia praecox. *Brit. M. J.*, **2:** 757–760, Sept., 1906.

———: Constructive formulation of schizophrenia, *Am. J. Psychiat.*, **1:** 355–364, No. 3, Jan., 1922.

———: The nature and conception of dementia praecox. *J. Abnorm. Psychol.*, **5:** 274–285, Dec., 1910.

Moersch, Frederick P., and James W. Kernohan: Hypoglycemia: neurologic and neuropathic studies, *Arch. Neurol. & Psychiat.*, **39:** 242, Feb., 1938.

Morse, M. E.: The pathological anatomy of the ductless glands in a series of dementia praecox cases, *J. Neurol. & Psychopath.*, **4:** 1, May, 1923.

Mott, F. W., and M. Prados y Suck: Some further pathological studies in dementia praecox, especially in relation to the interstitial cells of Leydig, *Proc. Roy. Soc. Med.* Sec., Psychiatry, **15:** 1, 1921.

———, and ———: Further pathological studies in dementia: pathological studies in dementia praecox, *New York M. J.*, **116:** 244, 1922.

Myerson, A.: Theory and principles of the "total push" method in the treatment of chronic schizophrenia, *Am. J. Psychiat.*, **95:** 1197, March, 1939.

———: Total push method, *Ibid.*, **96:** 935, Jan., 1940.

Naito, I.: Zur Frage der Zerebralen Fettsucht, *Arbeiten aus dem neurologischen Institute an der Wiener Universität*, **25:** 183–194, 1923–24.

O'Neill, Francis J.: Serious complications of insulin shock therapy, *Psychiatric Quart.*, **12:** 455, July, 1938.

Pavlov, I. P.: "Conditioned Reflexes and Psychiatry," New York, International Publishers Co., 1941.

Polatin, Phillip, Murray M. Friedman, Meyer M. Harris, and William A. Horwitz:

Vertebral fracture produced by metrazol-induced convulsions, *J.A.M.A.*, **112:** 1684, April 29, 1939.

Pollock, Horatio M.: Dementia praecox as a social problem, *State Hosp. Quart.*, **3:** 370–375, Aug., 1918.

———: Frequency of dementia praecox in relation to sex, age, environment, nativity and race, *Ment. Hyg.*, **10:** 596–611, July, 1926.

Raphael, T., J. P. Parsons, and M. N. Woodwell: Schizophrenic catatonia with associated metabolic and vegetative features, *Arch. Neurol. & Psychiat.*, **9:** 471–477, April, 1923.

Reese, Hans H., and Adrian Vander Veer: Protamine zinc insulin: its unsuitability for hypoglycemic shock therapy, *Arch. Neurol. & Psychiat.*, **39:** 232, Feb., 1938.

Romano, J., and F. G. Ebaugh: Prognosis in Schizophrenia, *Am. J. Psychiat.*, **95:** 583, Nov., 1938.

Ross, John R., and Benjamin Malzberg: A review of the results of the pharmacological shock therapy and the metrazol convulsive therapy in New York State, *Am. J. Psychiat.*, **96:** 297–316, Sept., 1939.

Sakel, M.: Therapy of schizophrenia by means of insulin hypoglycemia and hypoglycemic shock, *Wien. med. Wschnschr.*, **84:** 1211, Nov. 3, 1934; 1265, Nov. 17, 1934; 1299, Nov. 24, 1934; 1326, Dec. 1, 1934; 1353, Dec. 8, 1934; 1383, Dec. 15, 1934; 1401, Dec. 22, 1934; **85:** 35, Jan. 5, 1935; 68, Jan. 12, 1935; 94, Jan. 19, 1935; 121, Jan. 26, 1935; 152, Feb. 2, 1935; 179, Feb. 9, 1935.

———: A new treatment of schizophrenia, *Am. J. Psychiat.*, **93:** 829, Jan., 1937.

———: On the significance of the epileptic convulsion as a therapeutic factor in the pharmacological shock therapy of schizophrenia, *J. Nerv. & Ment. Dis.*, **87:** 140, Feb., 1938.

Somers, Donald C., and Robert P. Richardson: Bilateral fracture of femoral necks caused by metrazol convulsions, *Am. J. Psychiat.*, **95:** 1193, March, 1939.

Southard, E. E.: A study of dementia praecox group in the light of certain cases showing abnormalities of sclerosis in particular brain regions, *Am. J. Insanity*, **67:** 119–176, July, 1910.

Spielmeyer, Walter: "The Problem of the Anatomy of Schizophrenia," Assoc. Research Nerv. & Ment. Dis., **10:** 105–110, Baltimore, The Williams and Wilkins Co., 1931.

Strecker, E. A., and G. F. Willey: Analysis of recoverable dementia praecox reactions. *Am. J. Insanity*, **3:** 593–679, April, 1924.

———, and ———: "Prognosis in Schizophrenia," *Proc. Assoc. Research Nerv. Ment. Dis.*, **5:** 403–31, (1925) 1928.

Strecker, H. P., and M. D. Wurz: Recent advances in insulin therapy, *J. Ment. Sc.*, **84:** 146, Jan., 1938.

Tillotson, Kenneth J.: The practice of the "total push" method in the treatment of chronic schizophrenia, *Am. J. Psychiat.*, **95:** 1205, March, 1939.

Veer, A. H. Vander, and H. H. Reese: The treatment of schizophrenia with insulin shock, *Ibid.*, **95:** 27, Sept., 1938.

Weil, Arthur, Erick Liebert, and Gert Heilbrunn: Histopathologic changes in the brain in experimental hyperinsulinism, *Arch. Neurol. & Psychiat.*, **39:** 467, March, 1938.

Whitehead, Duncan: Improvement and recovery rates in dementia praecox without insulin therapy, *Psychiatric Quart.*, **12:** 409, July, 1938.

Williams, Guy H., Guy H. Williams, Jr., Helen M. Kingsbury, and David E. Bixby: Experience with pharmacological shock treatment of schizophrenia, *Am. J. Psychiat.*, **95:** 811, Jan., 1939.

Wortis, Joseph, and Richard H. Lambert: Irreversible or hyperglycemic insulin coma, *Am. J. Psychiat.*, **96:** 335, Sept., 1939.

SCHIZOPHRENIA (DEMENTIA PRAECOX

General Characteristics of Schizophrenia.—In the "normal," "average" or socially well-adjusted individual we find a certain orderliness and harmony in the mental life. The various expressions of the personality blend into a coherent, composite picture. Thought is logical, feeling is congruous, action more or less expedient and fitting, and sentiments are characterized by a subtle blending of affect and idea. There is such a synthesis of these different aspects of the personality that they seem to create a harmonious dynamic system of cognitive, affective, conative and constitutional forces. We are so accustomed to this harmonious blending of activity, emotional manifestation, ideational content and other expressions of personality organization on the part of our acquaintances that a serious lack of such agreement seems almost inconceivable to one not familiar with abnormal psychology. As we come to study mental diseases, however, we find a group of psychotic reactions characterized by disturbances in the harmonious blending and coördination of the various elements and aspects of the personality. In this disorder of personality functional mood tends to be inappropriate, thought disorderly and behavior maladaptive. Some parts of the disorganized personality system continue to function in relation to reality while others do not. Contributing to the complicated and variable personality disorder is a tendency to the development of disorganizing phantasy states and to an autistic withdrawal of self with resulting deterioration of habits.

History of Schizophrenia.—Although not so called the clinical picture we now know as schizophrenia has long been recognized. In 1849 John Conolly of Hanwell (England) Asylum, the champion of "no restraint," stated in his Croonian Lectures: "Young persons not infrequently fall into a state somewhat resembling melancholia, without any discoverable cause of sorrow, and certainly without any specific grief; they become indolent or pursue their usual occupations or recreations mechanically and without interest; the intellect, the affections, the passions, all seem inactive or deadened and the patients become utterly apathetic."

The term dementia praecox was first used by the Belgian psychiatrist Morel in 1860 in the case of a boy of fourteen who previously had always been "first in his examinations, and that without effort and almost without study . . . Unconsciously he lost his cheerfulness and became somber, taciturn, and showed a tendency to solitude." The boy showed a "state of melancholy depression and a hatred of his father even with the idea of killing him . . . . The young invalid progressively forgot all that he had learned, and his brilliant intellectual faculties entered into a very disturbing period of arrest. A kind of inactivity bordering on stupidity replaced his former activity and when I saw him again it looked as if a transition into an irrecoverable state of dementia praecox was taking place."

Unfortunately, Morel interpreted this disorganization of personality as an arrest of development to be included with mental deficiency as a "variety of intellectual, physical and moral degeneracy" due to heredity.

The next step in the history of dementia praecox was Hecker's description in 1871 of hebephrenia although the term had previously been used by Kahlbaum. "The characteristic features of hebephrenia," wrote Hecker, "above all are: its appearance in connection with puberty, the succession or changing appearance of various forms (melancholia, mania and confusion), the very quick termination in a psychic enfeeblement, and a characteristic form of final deterioration the evidences of which can be seen in the first stages of the disease."

Another step in the development of the dementia praecox concept was the description of catatonia by Kahlbaum in 1874. He described catatonia as "that condition in which the patient sits quietly or completely mute and motionless, immovable, with a staring countenance, the eyes fixed on a distant point and apparently completely without volition, without any reaction to sensory impressions, sometimes with a full fledged cerea flexibilitas as in catalepsy."

In 1896 Emil Kraepelin (1856–1926), often referred to as the great systematist of psychiatry, offered the proposition that a common denominator exists among such apparently unrelated syndromes as the hebephrenia of Hecker, the catatonia of Kahlbaum and many paranoid psychoses.

In 1906 Adolf Meyer (1866–) began to develop the thesis that dementia praecox is not a disease entity but rather a type of reaction developing in certain personalities as a result of progressive difficulty in adaptation and that the accumulation of faulty habits of reaction lead to a "habit deterioration."

Another landmark in the history of dementia praecox was the introduction by Eugen Bleuler (1857–1939), in 1911, of the term "schizophrenia." During the past twenty-five years there has been an increasing tendency to supplant the designation dementia praecox by the name schizophrenia (splitting of the mind) since the fragmentation of the psychobiological expression of the organism which we call mind, and the breaking up of a former normal synthesis of thought, feeling and activity, are now considered more characteristic and distinctive of the reaction than are symptom-complex and outcome as stressed by Kraepelin.

In the previous paragraph the term "reaction" rather than "disease" was used since it is increasingly agreed that the diagnosis "schizophrenia" is applicable not to a disease entity but to heterogeneous types of behavior tending to allied and serious disorganizations of the personality.

CONCEPTS OF SCHIZOPHRENIA

Since present concepts of schizophrenia are largely based upon the formulations of Kraepelin, Bleuler and Meyer a brief presentation of their respective formulations is added.

Kraepelin, through his keen observations, gave an excellent clinical description of the disorder while Bleuler and Meyer greatly advanced the psychiatric understanding of schizophrenia by their interpretation in dynamic terms of the symptomatic manifestations observed.

Kraepelin's Formulations.—As previously indicated Kraepelin brought together varied mental syndromes which he concluded were manifestations of a single disease entity to which he gave the name dementia praecox, a term previously having a more limited application. He thought these clinical syndromes arose from the same disease process since they had in common the following features: a beginning in adolescence or early adulthood; a progression toward a similar state of dementia; similar morbid processes were, Kraepelin assumed, the causes of the various clinical features. These causes, he assumed, might be either a degenerative disease of the brain or metabolic disturbances that produced auto-intoxication. Kraepelin believed that the clinical results of this process consisted of a weakening of emotional and volitional reactions and a loss of harmonious connections among emotional, volitional and intellectual reactions. He gave an extremely comprehensive and lucid description of the clinical features of dementia praecox but was critical of any attempt to explain the behavior of the patient on a psychological basis. Kraepelin divided dementia praecox into four types, a classification which many psychiatrists continue to attempt to use in spite of the difficulty in forcing many cases into one of these types.

Bleuler's Formulations.—Bleuler objected to the term dementia praecox because the illness does not necessarily begin in early adolescence nor invariably terminate in dementia. As previously indicated he introduced the term "schizophrenia" based on his concept that the personality is split up into different personalities through the influence of complexes. Bleuler believed that schizophrenia is a toxic or structurally determined process with histological alterations such as a decrease in the number of ganglion cells and changes in the glia. Organic processes, he suggested, cause the psychosis but psychogenic factors shape the clinical picture it assumes. Unlike Kraepelin, Bleuler, in spite of his conviction that schizophrenia has a somatic background, considered it to be a group of syndromes and not a disease entity. According to him this organic trouble manifests itself at the psychological level by a triad of basic disorders: (1) disturbances of association of ideas leading to incomprehensible, incoherent productions. This disturbance Bleuler regarded as the most fundamental. (2) Disturbances in affectivity with indifferent or unnatural expression of emotion. (3) Disturbances in relationship with the external world, an affective detachment from reality. As a result the schizophrenic has little or no rapport with the environment and lives in a world of his own with fantasies fulfilled or with feelings of being persecuted.

Bleuler distinguished two groups of symptoms in schizophrenia. One group he regarded as fundamental or primary, the other as secondary. He believed that disturbances of association and of emotion and ambivalence were primary and preceded the secondary ones in appearance. As corollary to these primary disturbances he included disorders of perception, apperception, consciousness, orientation, memory, reality appraisal, attention and will. As secondary symptoms he listed sensory illusions, delusions, catalepsy, stupor, negativism, mannerisms, automatism, impulsive acts and confusion.

Although Bleuler considered that schizophrenia has a physical basis yet he taught that it has a psychodynamic psychopathology based on a psychological background. The schizophrenic personality, according to Bleuler, is controlled by his inner life—by repressed memories and ideas heavily loaded with emotion, *i.e.*, by complexes which shape but do not cause the clinical picture. Meyer, perhaps justifiably, criticizes Bleuler's theory as assuming an unwarranted dualism of mind and body.

Meyer's Formulation.—Meyer's more dynamic conception of schizophrenia and his naturalistic behavioral approach in its formulation appeared earlier than Bleuler's work. He emphasized the clinical picture of schizophrenia not as an autonomous disease entity but as a type of reaction in certain personalities as a result of conflicts or complexes and a progressive difficulty in adaptation. He expresses the opinion that the failure to find any structural or physiological changes in neurones excludes an organic etiology. He calls attention to the disharmonies and deterioration of habit as one of the fundamental characteristics of the reaction. Meyer regards schizophrenia as the end-result of faulty habits of reaction, a progressive maladaptation of the patient to his environment with a final withdrawal from reality. He was one of the first to emphasize that the interest should be not so much in a classificatory diagnosis as in the facts and factors at work in the individual patient and in his assets. While admiring Kraepelin's description of the reaction Meyer does not subscribe to his invariably unfavorable prognosis of a progressive intellectual deterioration. As schizophrenic reactions Meyer would include "disturbances developing in particular constitutional types and expressed in vague, autistic fancy, projections, passivity, paranoid systemization, formal disorders of language and behavior, incongruity of affect and motivity disturbances." He further describes schizophrenic reactions as "twists and fundamental or fancy-born incongruities more or less foreign to average mature waking life." Because of the close identification of the term schizophrenia with dementia praecox Meyer prefers the term "parergasia," meaning thereby distorted or "twisted" behavior, performance or psychobiologically integrated behavior. While etymologically descriptive this designation has not been generally adopted. His formulation of schizophrenia has contributed greatly to a dispelling of the artificial dichotomy of mind and body and to the establishment of the proposition that mental disorder is a function of biological behavior.

Through his adaptation of the word-association test (page 479) devised by Galton, Jung contributed much to the theory of the psychogenic origin of schizophrenia. Its use may enable one to ascertain emotional problems to which the patient was unable to adjust successfully.

CAUSES

Anthropologically-minded psychiatrists point out that certain types of physique, temperament and energy direction appear to be associated with a frequency to be regarded as significant, thereby suggesting that the constitution and vital processes of the organism tend to produce specific, correlated forms of bodily structure and mental reactions. In their opinion the prepsychotic personality characteristics of the schizophrenic are so frequently associated with the leptosome, athletic or dysplastic physique, with the schizoid temperament and with introversion that a specific relationship must exist between physical constitution and personality organization in schizophrenia. While such a correlation seems at times to be present it by no means exists in all instances. A discussion of the alleged interrelated physical and personality characteristics of the schizoid was presented in Chapter VI, Psychobiological Constitution and Reaction Types, and will therefore not be repeated at this point. A large percentage of schizophrenic disturbances occur in persons who have been "shut in," have presented a barrier of remoteness and have withheld themselves from spontaneous emotional relationship with others. The resulting situation has been one of separateness, self-concealment and psychological isolation within which the patient has maintained an autonomous inner emotional life. Many such preschizophrenics have been inclined to indulge in vague, autistic fantasies and empty ambitions. Because of their emotional and social maladjustments and inadequacies they have been especially susceptible to schizophrenic reactions.

Although heredity and innate constitution, neuropathologic changes and disturbances in biochemistry and physiology are still discussed as etiologic agents yet the trend is to stress psychogenic factors. Various neuropathological changes have been described but none has been sufficiently uniform or typical to enable one to make a diagnosis under the microscope. Doubtless in many instances factors which superficially appear to be hereditary are in fact inherent in the environmental background in which the patient developed. Early warping in relationships with people significant in the environment of infancy or childhood may be important. Daily contacts with psychotic, eccentric or unstable parents or with other maladjustments in the family subjects the child to many unwholesome and pathogenic factors that predispose to subsequent mental disorders. There is reason to believe that environmental factors are extremely important in the development of personality features that predispose to schizophrenic disorganization.

If, as is the present trend of opinion, schizophrenia represents a special type of personality disorganization, a maladapted way of life manifested by one grappling unsuccessfully with environmental stresses and internal difficulties, its causes are to be found in the basic personality of the individual and the limits of his adaptive power, in the experiences which life has brought him and in the mental mechanisms and patterns of reactions by which he has attempted to deal with his special problems—faulty methods which constitute the symptoms of the disorder. It is now recognized that there is a continuous transition in behavior between the methods of dealing with sexual and other instinctive urges, with persistent childhood attitudes and phantasies and with social cravings and requirements on the part of persons whom we meet daily and the caricatures of these methods manifested by the schizophrenic. The same complex forces that predetermined the prepsychotic personality play also an important role in determining the clinical picture of the psychosis. To understand the etiology of a schizophrenic disorder in a given person and to formulate a diagnosis in psychobiological, dynamic terms it is first necessary to know his particular life history as fully as possible. One will therefore seek to formulate the clinical picture of schizophrenia in terms of the familiar problems and forces of human life rather than those of an impersonal disease entity. Only through a careful analysis of the personality and its evolution, of an equally detailed study of the concatenated life events and subjective experiences of the individual are the causes of the psychosis to be found, its manifestations understood and its psychological connections discovered and formulated. Among these factors are early conditioning experiences, intrapsychic conflicts, insistent but consciously rejected demands of various instinctive drives and urges, feelings of guilt or of insecurity, as well as various other long-standing, troublesome problems and frustrated purposes. In the adolescent, particularly, there may be a conflict between an artificial and perfectionistic code of morals on the one hand and intensifying sexual impulses on the other. Again there may be increasing rebellious tendencies or a growing realization of unfavorable comparisons with one's fellows. The patient's system of ideals may be too rigid to permit any reconciliation with gross instinctual impulses or to tolerate an increasing awareness of inferiority in competition. Attempts at solution become symptoms of the mental illness. Attempts to repudiate instinctual impulses may lead to autistic reverie, to withdrawal from interpersonal relationships and perhaps to self-punitive measures.

In addition to such specific factors we often have to do with a complicated personality imperfectly organized and inadequately prepared for the life experiences to be confronted, inclined to give up the struggle with reality, manifesting evasive and substitute ways of meeting problems, reacting to handicaps with oversensitiveness and tending to secure satisfactions, not from the real world, but from a subjective world of the individual's own making. Most persons who develop schizophrenia have failed to advance to mature, adult types of social and personal adaptation and integration. Overdependence upon the mother who may be reluctant to emancipate her child may prevent such a development of personality as is necessary for occupational, marital and social adjustments. Other traumatic and frustrating environmental influences, especially those that arise in the family constellation and contribute to uncertainty, insecurity and immaturity may lead to the development of personality liabilities that promote schizophrenic maladjustments. Frequently problems have been met by suspiciousness, bizarre beliefs and cults or by neurotic complaints. Not rarely the schizophrenic, long before the development of his psychosis, has felt that no one understood his lonely, unhappy personality. Underneath he may have been daydreaming, hating, fearing and perhaps despairing. In the opinion of many psychiatrists schizophrenia is so much the product of the personality that they question the propriety of speaking of it as a disease.

The *age of onset* ranges from late childhood to late middle age although the most frequent age is adolescence and early adult life. While uncommon yet it is not as rare in children (5 to 13 years) as formerly believed. The more fully the previous history is taken the more frequently will one find not merely the previous manifestation of schizoid traits but even of phenomena that were nearly or quite psychotic in nature. The high incidence during adolescence is not unnatural. There is probably, however, no specific relationship between dementia praecox and the puberty period. It is normally a period of personality discordance, of emotional cross currents and of struggle to adapt emergent, maturing urges to the demands of a restraining world. The individual is then precipitated into a critical emotional period without preparation or understanding. The adolescent is perplexed by sex, religious, vocational and social problems. He may be plagued by a desire for independence or crippled by a too prolonged dependence. The self-consciousness, the sensitiveness, moodiness, vague yearnings, sudden outbursts, defensive attitudes, the tendency to indulge in strange fancies, to project one's inadequacies and to be irritable are traits often particularly marked in adolescence. Frequently, especially in its early course, one meets with similar characteristics in schizophrenia. A certain number of prepsychotic schizophrenic personalities are attracted by a cloistered life.

FREQUENCY

Schizophrenia is one of the most frequent forms of the major psychoses, constituting from 15 to 20 per cent of the first admissions to public hospitals for mental diseases. Because the disorder tends to chronicity and in many instances does not shorten life it will usually be found that 60 per cent of the population of state hospitals is made up of schizophrenics.

SYMPTOMS

While there is a striking contrast between a normal, well integrated individual and the person reacting with a malignant form of schizophrenic psychosis yet frequently there is no abrupt transition from the schizoid type of personality to the manifest psychosis. Certain disharmonies of thought, of habits and of interests may have long existed. In adolescence there may have been a tendency to loneliness and perhaps to slight depressions. There may have been a vagueness of thinking, a tendency to projection of topics touching a special personal sensitivity and perhaps a tendency to be jealous of those more happily adjusted. As seen in the institution for mental diseases even the so-called "early" case of schizophrenia has frequently been becoming mentally sick for a considerable period before reaching the mental hospital, although the patient's family has not usually appreciated the nature or significance of any personality change. The *mode of onset*, except in the catatonic type, is often a gradual evolutionary process and there may be a transitional phase of a year or two. At this early stage there may be no single symptom that is pathognomonic of the disease. The impoverished, rigid affect of later stages has not yet appeared. A common early symptom is a withdrawal from interpersonal experiences and the development of a self-sufficient attitude. Instead of mingling with others the patient remains at home where he may show an increasing indifference to members of his family, to accustomed interests and to the demands and opportunities of his environment. There is a shallowness of affect and an impairment in richness and variety of emotional expression. A loss of appreciation of conventional values is noted. An insidious change in mood and outlook takes place. The patient seems preoccupied and his friends may speak of him as appearing "far away." Acquaintances attribute his loss of spontaneity, of ambition, of interest in competition with his group and of sustained effort in pursuit of former goals to laziness. An irritable discontent is common. The patient easily feels slighted and may begin to believe that others do not care for him or are talking about him. He may become ill at ease, restless, taciturn and wonder what interpretations others are putting on his behavior. A superficial attitude of superiority is not uncommon. Less heed is paid to social amenities and social requirements while former loyalties and affections become blunted. Frequently the patient becomes neglectful of personal care and cleanliness. Ruminations on sexual topics are not rare. The patient may feel that something wrong or unusual is going on in his environment. Mysterious meanings are discovered until finally misinterpretations and suspicions may cause him to move from place to place. For a few weeks or months the new environment may be free from any suggestion of hostility then the patient begins to feel that people are watching him or conspiring against him. Odd mannerisms or ways of acting may appear but they cause the patient no concern. Some patients express undue worry over their physical condition. This is especially suggestive of an approaching schizophrenia when the complaints are unusual or unlikely. The patient may add that he feels he should build himself up by means of dieting and exercise. The early schizophrenic is often preoccupied with abstract speculations or with metaphysical ponderings on such subjects as creation and causality, or with religious doubts, mysticisms and meaningless problems. A young colored truck driver who had but a seventh grade education wrote an essay entitled, "The Imperative Mind." In the very early stages, usually terminated before they reach a hospital for mental diseases, a few patients recognize that their ideas of reference and other abnormal mental experiences are unnatural; they may wish to know the meaning of their experiences and to understand their problems. Occasionally they may have some appreciation of the causes that have led to their illness. At this time they may be willing to discuss their problems. Later this desire is lost and the patient becomes inaccessible while in many the desire never existed. During these early stages before the construction of an elaborate symbolic system that becomes accepted as reality the conflicts are much less disguised and may often be discovered without difficulty.

As we pass from this initial, and what might be called premonitory stage or stage of incubation, to the manifest psychosis there appear an apparent *poverty and disharmony of feeling tone.* The dulling of finer feelings and an insidious narrowing of interests noted in the incipient stages become progressive. As the disease progresses and the emotional impoverishment increases the patient becomes indifferent, not merely to those sentiments and intangible values that make life worth living for the person in mental health, but, apparently existing at a vegetative level, he may be unconcerned as to fundamental comforts and needs. A few patients show, not an absence of mood, but a definite, prevailing one, such as euphoria or depression. The persistent mood, or emotional rigidity, has no relation to external circumstances or experiences and little or none to conscious mental content.

The other disturbance of affect is an emotional disharmony, often first exhibited by inappropriate smiling or laughing and silly giggling. Frequently the disharmony is between mood and conscious idea; there may, for example, be but little subjective feeling of depression even when ideas of despondency are expressed. At times experiences and ideas that should evoke a certain emotional response will produce its opposite—an emotional disconnection or dissociation. The patient, for example, may with a silly laugh speak of the death of his beloved mother. Whenever there is a display of affect by the schizophrenic it seems superficial, unnatural and stilted, quite lacking in any infectious quality. At times one observes capricious, fitful, apparently causeless changes in affect and mood. This inferior affective capacity, the deterioration and impoverishment of emotional expression and the inadequate and inappropriate emotional responses to situations constitute one of the important ways in which the personality is disorganized or split, and attest the aptness of Bleuler's designation of schizophrenia.

One of the most generally accepted hypotheses advanced as an explanation of this serious disturbance in the affective life of the patient is that the affect, contrary to first impression, is not lost or destroyed but is withdrawn from the conscious, perceptive aspects of the patient's life, from matters of objective reality, and attached to complexes and other material in the unconscious. As may happen to the financial world's credit the affect of the schizophrenic becomes "frozen." The affect is hidden, because fixed in special, limited constellations of ideas. According to this theory the disorganization or disorderliness of affect appears all the greater because it is associated with and determined not by one constellation of unconscious ideas but by many complexes among which there may be active conflict and discord. Since the affect is attached to and determined by material that is inaccessible the emotions appear out of harmony with the contents and expressions of consciousness, although they are really in harmony with the psychic material to which the affect is attached and by which they are governed. The emotional disturbance in schizophrenia may therefore not be really a deterioration but a displacement.

The emotional apathy of the schizophrenic may perhaps be theoretically explained in a somewhat different manner. One way by which the normal person may deal with difficult and threatening situations is by minimizing or ignoring them. It is conceivable, therefore, that the emotional dullness and indifference of the schizophrenic is a defensive reaction to all life. Although this blunting of feeling arose as a mechanism of defense against a definite troublesome situation in the inner world of the patient it irradiates and becomes a general behavior pattern of the personality. When interest and affect are withdrawn from the conscious, familiar material with which they were formerly connected and are attached to the content of the unconscious a state known as *depersonalization* may exist. In this the individual feels himself changed throughout in comparison with his former state. As a result he no longer acknowledges himself as a personality. His actions seem mechanical and automatic and he observes them as if a spectator. The patient does not believe he is another personality (transformation of personality) but has rather a sense of loss of the limits of his own personality with its directive ego. The identification of one's own personality may become indistinct or confused. It seems to the patient that he no longer has any internal self to which he can refer forces and influences. In his attempt to rationalize this sense the patient may come to feel that parts of his body or his mind seem strange and as though not belonging to him. He may develop more nihilistic ideas and believe that he no longer has a body, that there is no world, or that he is dead. In addition to this change of self there may be a change in the environment which seems strange to the patient and to have lost its character of reality. States of unreality are probably closely related to thought block, feelings of stupidity, fugues, dream states and other involuntary withdrawals.

Among the disturbances of affect in schizophrenia one occasionally meets with hypochondria. Sometimes this depressive preoccupation with subjective bodily feelings seems to have for its purpose the exclusion of a disturbing contact with the problems of reality. Again a sort of vicarious relief is afforded if that which is troublesome within, a sense of guilt, for example, is expressed in terms of distress of the body for the processes of which the patient does not feel responsible. Bodily complaints are mainly present at the beginning of schizophrenia and later disappear. Frequently these complaints are bizarre or peculiar, such as that there is a sense of electric currents in the genitals or that the body is becoming smaller.

One result of the schizophrenic's loss of capacity for attachment of energy and interest to external objects and reality and of its affixture to his subjective life and its experiences is a *narrowing of attention*. Interest, and therefore attention, is centered on subjective creations, on matters within and not without the patient. This lack of attention and of concentration gives rise to the misleading impression that the patient is intellectually impaired whereas he is intellectually inert. The replies of the schizophrenic are often trivial and uninformative because interests and energy are directed toward material not accessible to ordinary questioning. *Paralogia*, a condition in which the patient's reply shows that the question has been understood, but the answer to which, because of defective reasoning, is erroneous, is due to the dereistic thinking to which the schizophrenic is particularly given.

While active attention—concentration—as just indicated, is often disturbed, yet passive attention is much less affected with the result that while the patient may be living in a world of phantasy he is still able to maintain a contact with reality sufficient for certain practical needs, yet often too inadequate for a socialized adjustment. Schizophrenics may be perplexed but probably do not suffer from disturbances of the sensorium and therefore from confusion in the correct sense of the term.

From what has been said it will be seen that there is rarely a dominant affect in schizophrenia as is the case in manic-depressive psychosis. On the contrary there are numerous inharmonious affects arising from conflicting desires and complexes, or the affect may be fixed to or absorbed by phantasies, by elaborate symbolic systems and other products of the unconscious. The result is a disorderliness and apparent impoverishment of affect that contribute to the peculiar disorganization of personality which characterizes the schizophrenic.

Normally *associations of ideas* follow one another with a definite logical connection, progressing to an ultimate completeness of thought, but in schizophrenia they may be shortened, fragmented, and otherwise so disturbed as to lack logical relationship. Although the disturbances of associations in schizophrenia do not become particularly marked until serious disorganization of the personality has taken place, yet not rarely one finds that long before any manifest psychosis developed the patient's thinking had been involved and had shown odd sequences of ideas. Later he may employ generalities so vague that they convey no meaning to the average person. Doubtless, however, the communications of the schizophrenic are nearly always self-meaningful although often their significance is not grasped by others. One of the earliest symptoms observed by the psychiatrist may be a certain inconsequence and odd sequence of ideas. There is a slight irrelevancy as if the patient has missed the point. As the disease becomes established there is a tendency for associative connections to become incongruous, at times becoming so broken or incomplete that the patient's utterances become fragmentary, disconnected, illogical or even unintelligible. Some use such abstract words that precision in meaning is lacking. The use of eccentric metaphorical expressions is also common. Set phrases may come to be used repeatedly as stereotypes. The use of neologisms by the mental patient always suggests a schizophrenic psychosis. These probably represent extreme condensation. This, in turn, may spring from dereistic thought. The thought productions of the schizophrenic often become characterized by vagueness, alliteration, condensation and unusual symbolism. Speech may show a curiously distorted use of language varying from a stilted and formal phraseology without apparent substance to a "word salad" of nouns and verbs having practically no articulated structure, or even without apparently meaningful connection. Doubtless there was earlier a significance which became lost. Affectations in manner of speech are often observed. The following is taken from a schizophrenic production entitled "Equalitized Metabolic Demention Metabolism":

"Improper wave length—wave length changes later visible death. That is a moving trollysis similar to circulation of life action. Born high focussating action may die through wave length charge and still live until visible death takes place.

"Education comes from radiation of action. Anyone can study all science in a compositive way. It takes a compositive mind to be able to understand. Can tell compositive minds by stromonized conception. The mind at birth takes on a birthification becomes environmental by the radiation to it. Metabolism to dimension differ in every person is of actions of metabolism and dimension balancing. . ."

How the thinking of a formerly well trained mind may become disorganized by the schizophrenic is illustrated in the following intellectualized rumination taken from a letter written by a man who had had a scholastically brilliant college career and after graduation had spent two years at Oxford as a Rhodes scholar:

"I'm too utterly weary from battling with my financial-religious and general-religious problems to be able to survive any shock of learning that unhintably hard-won progress supposed to have been earned in the fraternal-religious problem is illusory. For that would wreck me—in my critically exhausted condition—with horror lest humanity—contrarily from being faith-imbued joy-multipliers of Revelations All Embracing God or Unfathomably Progressive Universe—are duped victims of God's opposite faith-deluding us—with illusions of immortality, a Heavenly Father and of progress—into accommodating as evil-absorbers of His unconvertible and endless agonies and struggle."

There is probably no disturbance in the physical associative apparatus, the explanation for the disorders in the thinking of the schizophrenic being found in the great extent to which associations are directed by affective processes and by complexes. Because of these affect-toned complexes associations are broken, are led into bypaths, are fragmented, incongruous, do not progress, or are joined through common affects rather than through conscious, logical connection, with the result that various forms of incoherence follow. When the connections appear particularly loose we speak of the schizophrenic's thought as being "scattered." This means that the unconscious connection of ideas is unusually marked. This scattering is comparable to and is to be looked upon as having the same significance as free associations. There seems to be much, too, to suggest that the psychological processes operative in the associations of the schizophrenic are closely allied to the condensations, substitutions and other processes of dream-work in the normal person as discussed on page 484.

Many schizophrenics show a poverty of associations and of ideas due, presumably, to preoccupation with affective material having its source largely in the unconscious and to the accompanying narrowing of attention. To be ascribed to these two conditions, also, are the casual and trivial remarks and replies of the schizophrenic so peculiar to the disorder as to have important diagnostic significance.

Affective elements in repressed constellations of ideas may produce various ellipses, short-circuitings of ideas and even neologisms. These coined words are condensations and symbolizations of complexes, conflicts and other unconscious material highly charged with affect. Within their concealed meaning are compressed the condensations of words that refer to persons or things intimately related to the individual's particular conflict or psychic experience.

In connection with disturbances of associations mention should be made of the fact that in early schizophrenia a fairly typical flight of ideas may occur, which later tends to develop into incoherence.

Blocking may occur as associations approach painful conflict material. It results from an affective impediment of thought and tends to arise largely in connection with special topics whereas neutral topics may be handled as usual.

The thinking of the schizophrenic tends to become dereistic; associations and symbols are formed in the unconscious, are molded and directed by affective constellations and instinctive undercurrents. They then rise into consciousness where as dereistic thinking they constitute a type of thought much like that of dreams. It may show a tendency to symbolism, displacement and condensation. Dereistic thinking is a pleasurable thinking that tends to falsify reality and to disregard realistic, logical and scientific thought. It is not corrected by the logic of experience or by the demands of the external world.

Schizophrenic thinking is much like the prelogical thinking of children and of primitive man, both types tending to be paralogical in nature. In the undisciplined and imaginative thinking of the schizophrenic, of primitive man and that of the infant there seems, too, to be an absence of distinction between the external and the internal world. Ideas are often indistinctly and inexactly outlined. It has been shown by Rorschach test performances that what has been conceived as fantasy is really distortion, misconstruction and inaccuracy, but not fantasy in the sense of a new creation.

The dominant ideational content of the schizophrenic is often delusional in nature. Because the satisfactions sought by his beliefs are so highly disguised by their symbolism and because the needs in response to which the *delusions* have been created are often not apparent, the delusions of the schizophrenic often appear grotesque and meaningless. His delusions are never meaningless, however, but are specific and adapted to the peculiar psychological needs and situation of the individual and are in keeping with his particular life experiences. Although it is often difficult to ascertain there is always a relevance in the schizophrenic's ideas and symbols to the problems and purposes of his personality.

The tendency of the schizophrenic's delusions to be grotesque, to be loosely organized, to center around themes of persecution, of grandiosity and of sex, to arise from autistic sources and yet to be expressed in a relatively clear setting is shown in the following letter addressed by a patient to one of the male physicians connected with the hospital in which she was under treatment:

Dear Dr.—

"My Plan," or as mother used to call you, "The Little Plant," or else one little Plant for I was the other Plant, called "Tant." Will you please see that I am taken out of this hospital and returned to the equity court so I can prove to the court who I am and thereby help establish my identity to the world. Possibly you do not remember or care to remember that you married me May 21, 1882, while you were in England and that I made you by that marriage the Prince of Wales, as I was born Albert Edward, Prince of Wales. I am feminine absolutely, not a double person nor a hermaphrodite, so please know I am England's feminine king—the king who is a king.

Your first duty is to me, and if you do not intend to do the right thing, helping me to get out of here, stop the thefts of clothing, money, jewelry, papers, letters, etc., etc.; you will please let me know so I can make some absolute change and further demand of the nations my release.

1874 Building was to have been a palace for my mother, father, myself and you, that is, if you are the one I married—so why not get busy and furnish it up as such when I go abroad. Make my trips (our trips?) short and return to America on important matters and have the right place to hold court. You and Dr. Black can take me to the equity court where I prove up my individuality and this must be done.

Sincerely,
"Tant"

Queen of Scotland, Empress of the World, Empress of China, Empress of Russia, Queen of Denmark, Empress of India, Maharajahess of Durban, "Papal authority" as a Protestant.

In the early stages of schizophrenia the delusions may not be fixed and the patient may at times be in doubt as to his ideas of reference or as to the hostility of his environment; later he becomes convinced that his delusions are real facts. At the onset of his psychosis the schizophrenic may have obsessive ideas that prove to be the early stages of a process that later becomes frankly one of externalization and projection.

Delusions in the schizophrenic often serve rather effectually in subjectively reorganizing his life situations and in dealing with such problems as thwarted trends and drives, frustrated hopes, biological inadequacies, feelings of insecurity, disowned qualities, gnawing feelings of guilt and the affective constellations and other contents of the unconscious. In no other type of mental disorder are the patient's problems, wishes and conflicts so thoroughly dramatized and symbolized in fantastic form. This fact and the schizophrenic's impairment of his ability to appreciate and test the reality of his fantasies tends to the creation of extravagant and bizarre delusions.

There is a tendency to a reversion to belief in magical cause and effect.

In no other form of mental disorder do *hallucinations*, or the projection of inner experiences into the external world in terms of perceptual images, occur in the presence of clear consciousness so frequently as in schizophrenia. Their mechanism is not unlike that of hallucinations in other abnormal states but they tend to be more highly disguised in nature and to constitute a primitive form of adjustment and are therefore of much more serious significance than is their presence in delirium or in intense emotional disturbances. It is not difficult to conceive of highly significant material in the schizophrenic's inner life as assuming hallucinatory vividness. It is but a step from the figurative "voice of conscience" to its audible perception. Unconscious material and unadjusted tendencies break through and create sense perceptions, perhaps highly symbolized, in response to psychological needs and problems. Disowned desires and feelings of guilt are projected as auditory hallucinations which, as the voice of conscience, accuse and criticize. The patient, incapable of recognizing the origin or significance of his hallucinations, believes in the reality of these projected images, accepts them at face value and reacts in accordance with what he has accepted as reality. He can no longer distinguish between inner experience and the outer world. Hallucinations are not an early symptom of schizophrenia although in the absence of an adequate history they may appear so. As Freud points out they are not possible until the patient's ego is so far disintegrated that the testing of reality no longer stands in the way.

The schizophrenic may find his hallucinations so serviceable that he is unwilling to relinquish them with the result that they come to constitute one of his cherished means of adjustment and he becomes occupied, not with a real, but with an hallucinatory world protected from the disturbances of reality. His hallucinations may be said to collaborate with delusions in the development of the same theme, the one by means of image symbols, the other by ideas.

But little need be said in the way of description of hallucinations in schizophrenia. They are more frequently auditory than of any other sense. Visual hallucinations are not particularly frequent and tend to be limited to acute phases of the psychosis. During their early occurrence hallucinations are often accompanied by considerable emotional tension but as the disease progresses they may cause but little concern and exert less influence upon behavior.

Among important symptoms of schizophrenia are the *disturbances of impulse and conation*, of action tendencies or the striving aspects of the personality. Many of these odd, unexplained and sudden activities grow out of a lack of harmonious association and integration of strivings, affects and wishes—the existence of incompatible and frequently, also, of changing objectives.

The capricious, impulsive behavior of the schizophrenic is to be looked upon as due to an ambivalence of impulse, a contradiction of conative tendencies. The concept of ambivalence, or contradictory manifestations of impulse, of idea or of affect, is greatly stressed by Bleuler, and considered by him to be a fundamental symptom of schizophrenia. It rests upon the principle that the idea, impulse or affect, is its exact opposite. Many psychiatrists believe that the conscious rejection and denial of expression of a desire but its indirect and unrecognized expression through projection in the form of hallucination or delusion is a manifestation of the principle of ambivalence. At any rate we find in schizophrenia a peculiar association of contradictions in the functions of the mind. Ordinarily our behavior represents a working harmony between diverse desires, a resultant of the contrasting considerations, forces and motives prompting us. In schizophrenia, on the contrary, the two conflicting impulses, one, many believe, of conscious origin, the other of unconscious, control behavior in erratic sequence, or even struggle simultaneously to direct it. There is a failure of integration of motive forces. Ambivalence may be manifested by an unstable blending of love and hate with sudden unaccountable shifts in affection and hostility leading sometimes to impulsive episodes.

At times a schizophrenic may consciously resist a certain impulse but nevertheless carry it through into action. Unconscious and dissociated tendencies acting in this way give the patient a feeling of being forced or controlled. Hohman expresses the opinion that a feeling of being forced may be due to the fact that the phantasy world in which the schizophrenic patient lives, rejects and disowns the experiences of the world of reality. This feeling of being forced may permit the entertainment of thoughts or the indulgence in behavior which the socially determined standards of the individual would not permit but for which, with his feelings of being forced, the patient no longer recognizes any responsibility.

A common disturbance of activity in the schizophrenic is an avoidance of concrete or spontaneous activity, a loss of initiative and purpose and the development of a state of inaction sometimes designated as anergia. Energy is withdrawn from externality. This deterioration in habits of activity may perhaps best be considered as a loss of interest in, and a retreat from the world of reality, one of the means adopted by the schizophrenic in renouncing the world with which he cannot cope. While the normal person secures his satisfaction by expending his energy in relation to the world of reality such a way gives no satisfaction to the schizophrenic whose interest and strivings are progressively withdrawn from the outer world. He secures his satisfactions through phantasy and by means of a symbolic gratification of insistent strivings and primitive impulsions.

Another disturbance of conation is negativism which may manifest itself in a perversity of behavior in the form of antagonism to the environment, opposition to the wishes of those about him, and in more marked cases, in mutism, rejection of food, refusal to swallow or even to void urine. Presumably negativism may be an expression of hostility, of a desire to exclude reality or may result from ambivalence. Some psychiatrists look upon negativism as a manifestation of regression and find an analogy between the perverse reactions observed in its mild forms and the conduct of the spoiled child.

Although quite the opposite of negativism in certain of its objective manifestations one occasionally meets with a pathological suggestibility which seems to have for its object the same purpose as negativism may have—a lessening of disturbing contacts with reality. It is less disturbing for the reality-evading patient blindly and passively to accept and follow whatever the environment suggests than it is actively either to oppose or to initiate contacts with reality. He may, therefore, show an automatic obedience to verbal directions without reference to their appropriateness or significance. Instead of answering a question he may repeat it in a parrot-like manner—echolalia. Again he may at once imitate the movement of a person in his immediate environment—echopraxia. Obediently to follow the suggestion of the environment involves neither initiative nor substantial contact with reality and does not divert interest or energy to the world outside the patient. The waxy flexibility of the catatonic represents this passive acquiescence to suggestions to a degree that may lead the patient to ignore physical discomfort or pain, accompanied usually by a marked disregard of his environment. Among the disturbances of activity mannerisms and stereotypies occupy a large place in the clinical picture. Schizophrenic mannerisms are of a wide variety. They may consist of affectations of manner, speech, gait, etc. Others consist of grimaces, sniffing, blowing out the cheeks, wrinkling of the forehead, ticlike movements or elaborate methods of performing certain activities and constituting a sort of ritual. Some patients assume certain postures for years. Sometimes the lips are puckered and held protruded in what is known as "snout cramp." The bizarre behavior of the schizophrenic has a meaning for the patient although its purpose and value are often obscured by condensation and symbolization.

In schizophrenia there is relatively little impairment of consciousness, orientation or memory although because of lack of interest it is sometimes difficult to test these functions. One often secures incorrect replies in answer to questions as to orientation but these are due to negativism, to the habit of giving casual replies in order to avoid troublesome reality, or are occasionally due to a lack of attention associated with a certain falsification by hallucinations and delusions. Forgetting, inattention, distraction and imaginative thoughts are used by normal persons as expedients to overcome a disappointment; these are used by the schizophrenic patient, not as substitutive reactions, but as if he were in a rut of least resistance.

Because of the disturbance in the integrative functions of the personality leading, as it were, to a disturbance in fusion of cognitive, affective and conative mental elements the schizophrenic is often described as demented. This, however, is not a correct use of the word as there is no irreparable impairment of cognitive and *intellectual functions*. The result could be better described as a disintegration or disorganization of personality. This does not mean that judgment, the capacity for making conceptual inferences, is not impaired. The patient not only has no appreciation of the disorganization which his personality has suffered but his concepts as to personal welfare and social relationships and purpose are rendered faulty and unreliable by his introverted tendencies and his falsification of reality by delusions and hallucinations.

The performance of Stanford-Binet and similar intelligence tests by disorganized schizophrenics differs both qualitatively and quantitatively from that of subnormal persons of the same mental age level. In normal persons and in the mentally deficient the age levels at which failures and successes are intermixed are grouped fairly closely around the determined mental age level, but in disorganized schizophrenics as in many other psychoses which have led to deterioration there is usually a spread of failures and successes at a number of age levels above and below the determined one. This phenomenon is known as "scatter."

The psychoanalysts speak of schizophrenia as a narcissistic withdrawal and regression. From their point of view the individual goes back to the early narcissistic stages of libidinous development. He sacrifices the ego organization, and the state of mind has a meaning from the point of view of the id only. The super-ego is pushed aside and is without effective power. In the more severe schizophrenic reactions the regression is to primitive stages and is sufficient to provide satisfaction of the id. Remainders of the ego and of the super-ego functions are, however, usually present to some degree. The ego is deprived of its powers but is not destroyed. The psychoanalytic school speaks of schizophrenia not merely as a regression, but postulates the theory that there is a destruction of the capacity or transference.

Schizophrenia is not rarely accompanied by certain *physical symptoms*. One of the most frequent of these is a general disequilibrium of the autonomic nervous system. This is shown by cold, bluish hands and feet, blotchy skin and widely dilated pupils which, when tested by a strong light, may contract momentarily but quickly dilate again. Occasionally the cyanosis may be quite marked. Sometimes patients in a catatonic stupor who persist in standing about in an immobile manner develop a striking edema. Attacks of vertigo and of hysteriform and epileptiform seizures may occur, more frequently in the early stages. A certain number of patients show a lowered metabolism. Many patients lose weight during the acute phases of the disease. Those who enjoy a favorable outcome of a schizophrenic episode often show a marked increase in weight during convalescence. An increase in weight without a coincident mental improvement usually denotes an unfavorable prognosis. Lewis concluded from his necropsy material that a hypoplasia of the circulatory system exists to an abnormal frequency. For various reasons, such as asthenic physique, poor respiratory hygiene, prolonged contact with carriers, and a sedentary, confined mode of life, pulmonary tuberculosis is usually frequent in schizophrenia. In a roentgenographic examination of 7,466 patients at the Hudson River State Hospital Leonidoff found an 8.8 per cent incidence of clinically significant tuberculosis.

TYPES OF SCHIZOPHRENIA

In formulating his conception of dementia praecox, Kraepelin classified his cases into different varieties depending on the prominence of certain symptoms. While he described many forms they are usually grouped into but four types. Efforts to classify schizophrenic patients into specific categories have been relatively fruitless and the present tendency is not to attempt the division. More understanding is to be gained by studying the patient and his life history as an individual problem than as a representative of some vague classificatory division. Bearing in mind that the classification is artificial the four types usually recognized will be described and cases illustrating the more characteristic symptoms will be cited.

Simple Type.—In this type the most marked disturbances are of emotion, interest and activity. If hallucinations occur they are rare and fleeting while delusions never play an important role. The disorder is usually gradual in its onset and assumes the form of an insidious change of personality, the significance of which is not understood by the patient's friends. In adolescence a youth who has perhaps shown much promise begins to lose interest in school or occupation, becomes moody, irritable and indolent. Shallowness of emotions, indifference or callousness, and absence of will or drive are prominent features. Neither criticism by others nor chagrin of parents causes concern. Appreciation of esthetic and moral values is lost. The required period of training or apprenticeship in preparation for profession or skilled occupation is not completed. Many become irresponsible idlers, vagrants, tramps, prostitutes or delinquents. In the milder cases the social maladaptation is less serious but the patients are considered as neighborhood eccentrics and although intellectually unimpaired are capable only of performing some simple routine task under supervision. The patient remains uninterested in his environment and unimpressed by responsibilities.

A. R. was committed to the hospital when twenty-one years of age following his arrest for window-peeping. In describing his childhood characteristics the patient's family stated that he "was always a little hard to understand," but was a quiet boy who never entered into rough games. His school record was excellent and he always stood high in his class. At seventeen when in the fourth year of high school he was obliged, because of a long illness of his father, to leave school and secure gainful employment. He secured work with a large manufacturing company where he soon came to be considered the second best operative on a certain type of machine. For two years he worked steadily, seemed ambitious and appeared to have a normal and wholesome, but not marked interest in girls. At nineteen he gave up his position, had no interest in securing another and when asked if he worked he would reply, "What do I want to work for? I have a father and sister working and they are enough." He appeared quite self-satisfied and felt that he should have a position of importance. At about this time he was first arrested for peeping at women's bedrooms. Through the influence of his father the charge was dropped. He became careless of his personal appearance and remained unoccupied except for occasional periods when he set up pins in a bowling alley. One year ago he was again arrested but again was released on the intercession of his father. He came to say little unless addressed and grew antagonistic toward his father and sister. He would remain out until midnight and then come home, eat a large meal, read until 2 a.m. and sleep until noon. Finally after his third arrest for peeping he was committed to the State Hospital.

On arrival at the institution the patient was found to be of asthenic physique and slightly effeminate in appearance. His emotional responses were shallow and inadequate. He showed no concern over his situation, laughed about it in a silly manner and referred to his offense as "Just a foolish idea." His hospital residence was characterized by apathy, preoccupation and inactivity. During the summer he would at times take part in the patient's baseball games but in winter he refused ground parole privileges. He never expressed any delusions and denied hallucinations. At times he would be seen, apparently much preoccupied, walking alone about the hospital reservation, laughing to himself.

Such a case illustrates how at times an individual, perhaps, as seems true in the present instance, fundamentally deviated psychobiologically, is unable to complete the transition from adolescence to maturity with its adult heterosexual and social adjustments. There seemed to be a certain innate limitation to the personality while environmental circumstances contributed but comparatively little to its disintegration. Interest became largely withdrawn from the actual world, psychobiologic energy was absorbed by the subjective life and there was a diminished response to social demands. This does not mean that life situations and events or psychological reactions to mental events were not dynamic factors in this patient's personality disorganization but that, as often happens in the schizophrenic, it is difficult, even by attempts at mental exploration, to discover and evaluate these elements.

Hebephrenic Type.—The onset of this type is insidious and usually begins in early adolescence. Occasionally the onset is subacute and characterized by a depression that suggests an affective reaction. Silliness and incongruous or inappropriate smiling and laughter are usual. In general one may say that hallucinations are frequent, that the ideational content tends to take the form of phantasy or of fragmentary bizarre delusions rather than of elaborate or systematized beliefs. Associative processes are loose, speech is incoherent, neologisms are common and mannerisms are frequent. Regressive features are prominent, wetting and soiling are common and the patient eats in a primitive, unmannerly fashion. The patient comes to lead a highly autistic life; he becomes bafflingly inaccessible and greatly introverted, while the final disintegration of personality and habits is perhaps the greatest of any of the types of schizophrenia.

T. B., a single young woman of thirty-two when admitted to the hospital, may serve to illustrate the nature of certain of these unwholesome prepsychotic reactions as well as the symptoms and course of a malignant schizophrenia that might be considered of the hebephrenic type. Of her five children Theresa was her mother's favorite. Greatly petted and babied by her mother she always remained dependent upon her. She is described as being a pretty child with a rosy complexion. She early became aware of this fact and enjoyed dressing up and strutting about to display her good looks. In spite of these signs of vanity she was timid and shy and would blush in a self-conscious way when she realized that people were noticing her. In childhood she did not play freely with other children; "she thought herself above other children," and is described by her sisters as having in later years "a rather good opinion of herself and her abilities," and by her neighbors as "high hat." Soon after leaving school at sixteen she began to work in a bleachery where she remained until shortly before her commitment. She never had any girl chums and did not participate in the activities of other girls at her place of employment. Her attitude was one of "proud distance." While still in school there were several boys who were quite friendly toward her but her sister said she could remember no instance when the patient had any male callers or associates after she grew up, although she gave much attention to her clothes and personal appearance, obviously in the sister's opinion, in an effort to attract the attention of young men. Her family described her as devoid of humor, as sensitive, jealous, stubborn, willful, and easily angered. She become more seclusive, had "melancholy spells," became preoccupied, paid less attention to her environment, and when addressed would ask in an indifferent way, "What did you say?" She became irritable and critical particularly of the wife of her brother with whose family she lived. About six months before commitment she "began to grow thin and nervous," became careless about her work which deteriorated in quality and quantity. She believed that other girls at her place of employment were circulating slanderous stories concerning her. She complained so indignantly that X., an attractive young man employed in the same industrial plant, had put his arm around her and insulted her that her family demanded that the charge be investigated, with the result that it was not only shown that the charge was without foundation but that the young man in question had not spoken to her for months. The family, however, had not suspected mental disease until six days before her commitment when she returned from her work. As she entered the house that evening she laughed loudly, watched her sister-in-law suspiciously, refused to answer questions and at sight of her brother began to cry. She refused to go to the bathroom saying that X. was looking in the windows at her. She ate no food and the next day declared that her sisters were "bad women," that everyone was talking about her, and that X. had been having sexual relations with her, that although she could not see him he was "always around." In her hallucinatory experiences she heard X. say, "Aren't you going to fire her? I've had her. She don't know it." The patient became resistive, was afraid of being killed, and at times said, "I'm dead." She stated that she was being poisoned, saw her dead mother and heard her speak. As the patient became noisy, did not sleep and ate but little and only when spoon-fed, she was committed to a private institution. Here she was uncooperative, silly, grimaced and whiningly repeated, "Oh, Mamma! Mamma! I want to see my father before I die." She heard voices outside her window and at night would come to the door of her room several times saying, "What is it all about? Oh, Mamma!" Her associations became loose, she took no interest in the care of her person or in other patients, but would stand for hours with her back against the wall, her head thrust forward, fingering her hair and unheeding her environment.

After a residence of four months in the private institution the patient was transferred to the State Hospital. As she entered the admitting office she laughed loudly and repeatedly screamed in a loud tone, "She cannot stay here; she's got to go home!" The patient grimaced and performed various stereotyped movements of her hands. When seen on the ward an hour later she paid no attention to questions although she talked to herself in a childish tone. She moved constantly about, walking on her toes in a dancing manner, pointed aimlessly about and put out her tongue and sucked her lips in the manner of an infant. At times she moaned and cried like a child but shed no tears. As the months passed she remained silly, childish, preoccupied, inaccessible, grimacing, gesturing, pointing at objects in a stereotyped way, usually chattering to herself in a peculiar high-pitched voice, little of what she said being understood. At an interview eighteen months after her hospitalization she presented an unkempt appearance, was without shoes, sat stooped far over, smiled in a silly manner and presented a picture of extreme introversion and regression. During the attempted interview she rarely spoke although she occasionally replied, "I don't know" in an entirely indifferent manner and apparently with no heed to the question. The nurse reported the patient as seclusive, resistive, idle and with no interest either in the activities of the institution or in her relatives who visited her.

Catatonic Type.—The catatonic type is characterized by phases of stupor or of excitement in both of which negativism and automatism are prominent features. These phases frequently alternate, perhaps with one phase changing suddenly to its opposite, although many times a given catatonic episode may present but one phase throughout its course. Again there may be an admixture of symptoms usually thought of as belonging characteristically to one or the other phase. The most frequent age of appearance is between fifteen and twenty-five. Of the various types of schizophrenia the catatonic most frequently has a somewhat acute onset and is oftenest precipitated or preceded by an emotionally disturbing experience. The prognosis for a recovery with reintegration of personality after a catatonic episode is more favorable than in the case of other types of schizophrenia, although after a period, perhaps after several episodes, there is a tendency for the catatonic type to pass over into states approaching hebephrenic or paranoid types with a permanent disorganization of the personality.

Catatonic stupor, or the stuporous phase, is often preceded by depression, discontent, or by emotional fermentation. The patient is inclined to be uncommunicative and his reactions become increasingly characterized by failing interest, inattention, preoccupation, emotional poverty and dreaminess. Mute, stuporous, and with masklike facies the catatonic may occasionally keep his eyes closed but more frequently he stares fixedly and blankly downward. He denies the world and actively resists the environment. He opposes any effort to move him from attitudes and positions, often constrained and peculiar, which he has assumed and may maintain for months. The patient refuses to dress or to eat, although occasionally if he thinks he is unobserved he will eat greedily. Saliva, urine and bowel contents are often retained. He may not only soil clothing but even exhibit an apparent purposefulness in his annoying disregard of all cleanliness in his habits of excretion. Gestures, grimacing and grinning are common. The hands may be held tightly clenched and other muscle tensions be maintained. Catalepsy, either flexible or rigid, may be present. In this state the patient initiates no spontaneous movements but maintains the postures into which he is passively impressed. Through automatic obedience the patient may carry out any verbal instructions, regardless of their absurd or even dangerous nature. He shows no reaction to feinting motions before the eyes, to pin pricks or to other painful stimuli. Although giving no indication whatsoever that he is at all aware of what is going on about him the patient really registers the events of his environment and when he begins to speak again he may give a surprisingly full account of incidents occurring in his stupor. In spite of the apparent ideational poverty there seems every reason to believe that ideas and representations are by no means absent, but rather centered about a dominant ideo-affective constellation. Perhaps an analogue to catatonic stupor may exist in the unapprehending, impassive response with which profound, overwhelming bereavement or catastrophe may at times be met. Both this reaction and the catatonic stupor of the schizophrenic may serve as methods of meeting situations too difficult to be met by active, resolute measures. Again the stupor may be compared to a retreat into an intense, trance-like preoccupation or reverie.

After a period of extremely variable duration the patient slowly, or at times suddenly, emerges from this stuporous state. Interest, affect and behavior may return more or less closely to normal, or the patient may pass into a state of catatonic excitement.

Catatonic excitement is characterized by an unorganized overactivity that is without emotional expression, is not influenced by external stimuli, is incoherent, apparently purposeless, stereotyped, confined to a limited space, and partakes of the nature of automatisms. Impulsiveness and destructiveness are frequent. Without warning or apparent cause, the patient may suddenly attack an inoffensive bystander or break a window. He destroys his clothing, remains nude and disregards all execretory cleanliness. Negativism is usually marked. The flow of speech may vary from mutism to a pressure suggesting a flight of ideas. Attitudinizing, mannerisms, sterotypies and grimaces are frequent. The patient may react to terrifying or ecstatic hallucinations of sight or hearing. Mystical experiences are not uncommon. Hostility and feelings of resentment are common. The patient may be sleepless, appear deliriod, refuse food and become dehydrated and exhausted. There is often a rapid loss of weight.

Probably acute catatonic excitement is often the same as the reaction which Kempf has termed acute homosexual panic. The great overactivity is often accompanied by fearfulness and auditory hallucinations that accuse the patient of homosexual practices or inclinations. As previously noted he is often assaultive.

Whether catatonic stupor should be interpreted psychologically or whether it should be explained on the basis of physical and chemical changes has been the subject of much dispute. Probably the present tendency is to regard it as an evasion of a life situation. The fact that the catatonic changes his postural rigidities during sleep as frequently as normal persons (Cheney) seems to show that it is of cerebral and probably of psychic origin rather then determined by toxins, endocrine imbalance, circulatory insufficiency or neuropathological changes in the cerebral cortex. Meyer considers that catatonia is a psychobiological reaction. Hohman quotes him as describing it as "closely related to what is seen in hypnotic states and in mystical fancies, and like stages in religious symbolism and feelings of submission to influence by mystic power." When the problems of life are too great we naturally seek death but are deterred from suicide by the instinct of self-preservation. Many psychiatrists, therefore, look upon catatonic stupor as a profound regression, a dramatization of death. Attention is called to the similarity between catatonia and the instinctive immobility reaction exhibited by certain animals when confronted with a life-threatening situation.

Mention should be made of the fact that catatonic reaction-types are observed in organic brain disease such as paresis, tumor, abscess, in toxic and exhaustive states, as well as in certain poorly understood psychoses of the presenile period. This, however, does not mean that psychological mechanisms may not also be operative in such cases.

The case of A. C., aged thirty-two, will illustrate many of the features observed both in the excited and the stuporous phases of catatonia:

The father was stubborn and self-willed, the mother was excitable and temperamental. At seven years of age he went to live with his grandparents. The grandfather whose "word was law," who suffered from epileptic seizures and subsequently died in a hospital for mental diseases, had no understanding of the child's point of view. His seizures greatly frightened the boy. The patient was a seclusive, daydreaming, timid, shy and sensitive but stubborn and self-willed child. He still remembers with resentment how his father whipped him before another boy whom he would not thank for an apple. He was uninterested in the play life of other children and spent his time either in the town library or in his own room where he made various toys which he guarded jealously from other children, allowing only his sister, his sole confidante, to share them. At seventeen he graduated from high school where he had learned easily but had taken no part in the extracurricular activities. His occupational history was without significance except for the fact that his early promise of success as a draftsman and designer of aeroplanes and motors had not been sustained and that for eight years prior to his commitment he had earned practically nothing. At twenty he married. Two months before commitment the patient began to talk about how he had failed, had spoiled his whole life, that it was now "too late." He spoke of hearing someone say, "You must submit." One night his wife was awakened by his talking. He told of having several visions but refused to describe them. He stated that someone was after him and trying to blame him for the death of a certain man. He had been poisoned, he said. Whenever he saw a truck or a fire engine the patient stated that it was looking for him in order to claim his assistance to help save the world. He had periods of laughing and shouting and became so noisy and unmanageable that it became necessary to commit him.

On arrival at the hospital the patient was noted to be an asthenic, poorly nourished man with dilated pupils, hyperactive tendon reflexes and a pulse rate of 120 per minute. In the admission office he showed many mannerisms, lay down on the floor, pulled at his foot, made undirected, violent striking movements, again struck attendants, grimaced, assumed rigid, attitudinized postures, refused to speak and appeared to be having auditory hallucinations. He was at once placed in a continuous bath where, when seen later in the day, he was found in a stuporous state. His face was without expression, he was mute, rigid, and paid no attention to those about him or to their questions. His eyes were closed and the lids could be separated only with effort. There was no response to pinpricks or other painful stimuli. On the following morning an attempt was made to bring him before the medical staff for the routine admission interview. As he was brought into the room supported by two attendants he struggled, grimaced, shouted incoherently and was resistive. For five days he remained mute, negativistic and inaccessible, at times staring vacantly into space, at times with his eyes tightly closed. He ate poorly and gave no response to questions but once was heard to mutter to himself in a greatly preoccupied manner, "I'm going to die—I know it—you know it." On the evening of the sixth day he looked about apparently astonished to find himself in the tub, and asked where he was and how he came there. When asked to tell of his life he related many known events and how he had once worked in an aeroplane factory, but added that he had invented an appliance pertaining to aeroplanes, that this had been stolen, patented through fraud and that as a result he had lost his position. He ate ravenously, then fell asleep and on awaking was in a catatonic stupor, remaining in this state for several days. He gradually became accessible and when asked concerning himself he replied that he had had "a nervous breakdown following the physical breakdown." He referred to his stuporous period as sleep and maintained that he had no recollection of any events during it. He said "When I was in the tub I didn't known anything. Everything seemed to be dark as far as my mind is concerned. Then I began to see a little light, like the shape of a star. Then my head got through the star gradually. I saw more and more light until I saw everything in a perfect form a few days ago." Two days later he admitted that he could remember having seen the examiner while in the tub. He rationalized his former mutism by a statement that he had been afraid he would "say the wrong thing," also that he "didn't know exactly what to talk about." From his obviously inadequate emotional response and his statement that he was "a scientist and an inventor of the most extraordinary genius of the twentieth century," it was plain that he was still far from well.

Paranoid Type.—The features which are particularly apt to occupy the foreground in this type or phase are delusions, often numerous, illogical and disregardful of reality, hallucinations, and the usual schizophrenic disturbance of associations and of affect together with negativism. The paranoid type tends to have its frank appearance at a somewhat later age than the other forms, perhaps most frequently from thirty to thirty-five. In the early stages the delusions are often limited but later they become numerous and changeable. In the early stages, too, their character usually indicates more clearly the particular psychological needs or experiences which they are created to meet. Occasional remarks may supply fragmentary disclosures of the patient's preoccupations. Rejected tendencies are ideationally projected instead of undergoing repression. Delusions of persecution are the most prominent in paranoid schizophrenia, but expansive and obviously wish-fulfilling ideas, hypochondriacal and depressive delusions are common. With increasing disorganization delusional beliefs become less logical. The patient is subjected to vague magical forces and his explanations become bizarre and fantastic. Imaginative fantasy may become extreme but take on the value of reality. Repressed aggressive tendencies may be released; some inarticulate paranoids may manifest an unpredictable assaultiveness. Many paranoid schizophrenics are irritable, discontented, resentful, suspicious and show a surly aversion to being interviewed. Some manifest an unapproachable, aggressively hostile attitude and may live in a bitter aloofness. Mannerisms, apathy or incoherence are common.

C. E. was committed to a mental hospital when forty-four years of age because he had become disturbed by his delusions and hallucinations and had been found wandering about the streets only half clad. He was born in Finland and but little could be learned concerning his early life. He had always been a quiet, reticent individual, somewhat alcoholic and had never married. For several years he had been suspicious, and for at least three or four years had expressed many strange ideas. He believed people were talking about him, became neglectful of his aged mother, grew dull and listless, and did practically no work. For three months prior to his admission he complained that the devil was sitting on his chest. He would look out the window and cry out that the devil was coming down the street. He complained of his heart and chest and said that an "electric stroller" was passing over his body. He heard voices that disturbed and frightened him. At night he became particularly apprehensive, often screamed and on several occasions ran out partly dressed. On arrival at the hospital admission office he was asked as to what was the trouble, whereupon he replied, "I didn't have no trouble. Only the crooks bother me with wires and the State property. I heard it last summer when I worked in the City Yard. They have worms in the head. You heard them; you hear them voices talking to you. You know since old times back they have those things under the ground. Some kind of machinery and they are blowing up people under the clothes." At the formal mental examination made a few days after his admission he expressed satisfaction with his surroundings, then proceeded to tell how the ward building had "belonged to the Swedes for over four hundred years." He then explained that "the old man" was "downstairs." When an attempt was made to learn the identity of the "old man" the patient replied that it was his great-great-grandfather. He then told how this ancestor, who was still alive, the patient declared, owned all the adjoining property, at the same time looking out the window and pointing to the other hospital buildings. He related how this ancestor talked to him and told him how the property belonged to him. In reply to an inquiry the patient stated that he often saw this progenitor who lived "in one of those steel things down in the ground. He lifts up the cover." After a few weeks the patient became restless, noisy, more careless about his appearance and developed the habit of expectorating on his bed at night. When asked for the reason for this unpleasant practice the patient replied, "By the tubes you know in the wall. They put that in my nose. I telephoned to my school-master last night. My wife (it will be remembered that the patient never married) is down here, and my daughter Stella. There are monks and nuns. They are in the wall bothering people all over the city, with glasses from 1752 in 1851 in ages. I have thirty nine million dollars invested in the bank in Providence and I have three millions in Stockholm. I married a Swedish princess, Tirra." These statements were made in an indifferent manner and with no evidence either of hatred or of pretension. The patient's face was expressionless, he did not mingle with other patients, would at times be noted talking to himself and usually either lay quietly on a bench or walked slowly and aimlessly about the ward.

SCHIZOPHRENIA IN CHILDHOOD

Schizophrenia rarely occurs before the age of twelve but many cases arising at a considerably younger age have been reported. In older children the clinical features are much like those occurring in adults, whereas in children they are fewer and simpler than in older patients. There is a lack of interest in and of spontaneous contact with the environment. The patient suffers a loss of the lively curiosity normally shown by children. The schizophrenic child fails to derive satisfaction from the ordinary events of life, is preoccupied with subjective matters and his affective contact with people is impaired. Many types of thinking are described but nothing characteristic is consistently found. Regressive return to more immature types of behavior such as infantile toilet and feeding habits are common, or even return to such primitive ones as playing with feces may occur. Delusions and hallucinations are of questionable and certainly of infrequent occurrence. Their absence is not significant in younger children. Bender considers that anxiety is the nucleus of the schizophrenic problem in the earlier stages of the disorder. She believes that the presence of a severe anxiety in a child, unaccounted for by a reality situation, is in itself suggestive of schizophrenia.

Potter[1] specifies the following criteria for the diagnosis of childhood schizophrenia:

1. A generalized retraction of interests from the environment.
2. Dereistic thinking, feeling and acting.
3. Disturbances of thought, manifested through blocking, symbolization, condensation, perseveration, incoherence and diminution, sometimes to the extent of mutism.
4. Defect in emotional rapport.
5. Diminution, rigidity and distortion of affect.
6. Alterations of behavior with either an increase of motility, leading to incessant activity, or a diminution of motility, leading to complete immobility or bizarre behavior with a tendency to perseveration or stereotypy.

In venturing a diagnosis of schizophrenia in childhood one must satisfactorily establish that the child enjoyed a period of life free from psychotic symptoms before he became mentally ill. The course may be either acute or chronic.

COURSE AND PROGNOSIS

Contrary to the opinion formerly held schizophrenia is no longer considered to be a unity in cause, course, and outcome. While the occurrence of a schizophrenic reaction must always be looked upon with apprehension yet a permanent disorganization of the personality does not invariably follow. Indeed it is now the opinion of many of the closest students of schizophrenia that an acute, rather clearly psychogenic schizophrenia may at times disappear without leaving any injury to the personality. Formerly its incurable nature and progressive course were implied in the definition of the disease and a favorable outcome was considered presumptive evidence of an error in diagnosis. Of course, the occurrence of an obviously schizophrenic reaction should make one

[1] Potter, H. W.: Schizophrenia in Children. Am. J. Psychiat., *12:* 1254, 1933.

exceedingly careful in predicting that a permanently inferior type of adjustment will not be substituted. In recent years, too, there has been an increasing recognition that the episodic nature of a psychosis may not exclude a schizophrenic quality, although it commonly occurs that a schizophrenic psychosis which is episodic in its early course ultimately becomes uninterrupted. In episodic schizophrenia the psychosis may be punctuated by remissions or apparently complete intermissions. In many instances the outcome should be characterized as "social recovery" rather than as "cured" or as full recovery. By this is meant that the patient is able to return to his previous social environment and to previous or equivalent occupation, but with minor symptoms and signs such as irritability, shyness, or shallowness of affective responses.

From what has been said it will be seen that in any given case the effect upon the personality and future adjustment of the appearance of a schizophrenic reaction may be quite uncertain. In some cases the course is continuously progressive; in others it is intermittent. More frequently it is a question of remissions and relapses which, although they from the first insidiously tend to undermine interests and habits, still permit periods of adjustment at a lower level for a considerable period of time. It is estimated that 40 per cent of schizophrenics who enter public mental hospitals or clinics recover or improve and the other 60 per cent fail to improve or suffer that permanent, malignant disorganization of personality somewhat inaccurately designated as deterioration. The age of onset is not of prognostic significance except that relatively late age offers a less favorable prognosis. Sex has no prognostic significance.

As highly desirable and important as it is, it is not yet possible, with our limited knowledge concerning the factors and processes involved, for the psychiatrist when confronted with an acute schizophrenia definitely to predict what the future course of the particular psychosis will be. It may be parenthetically commented that the physician whose psychiatric experience is confined to institutions tends to develop an unwarrantably pessimistic attitude toward prognosis. There are certain facts, however, which may serve as general guides in suggesting an opinion. It will usually be found true that if the psychosis represents an insidious development and unfolding of a previous schizoid personality the prognosis is unfavorable. Many such psychoses represent the culmination of a long period of unsatisfactory adaptation. The better adjusted the patient's prepsychotic personality, the more directly and confidently the patient has been accustomed to meet the problems and difficulties of life, the richer his interests, the more definite an external precipitating cause and the more rapid the onset the better the prognosis. A slow, insidious withdrawal is apt to lead to an irreversible disorganization of the personality. The prognosis is not influenced by the intelligence or previous education of the patient. An apparently "mild" case need not be an early one nor of favorable prognosis. The presence of a well-marked affective element is of hopeful significance although a hypochondriasis is not desirable. The presence of cyclothymic factors in the personality background renders the prognosis more favorable. The persistence of hallucinations after an initial emotional tension has subsided is not a favorable indication. If the psychosis has existed for a year without clear-cut signs of improvement a favorable outcome is scarcely to be expected although it is by no means unknown. Previous remissions should lead one to expect that a given episode will be followed by improvement. The longer the interval between attacks the better the prognosis. In many cases of schizophrenia regression is an important mechanism, so attempts are often made to base a prognosis on the depth of regression manifested by the patient. Infantile posture and behavior, while often of unfavorable significance, should not outweigh other considerations in forming an opinion as to prognosis.

A word should be said as to the prognosis in the different types. In catatonia the prognosis is relatively good if the onset has been stormy and the episode is still acute. Many of these cases are restored to their prepsychotic level of adjustment for varying periods, at times for several years. The prognosis in the simple form with its insidious marasmus of the personality, developing in the absence of unusual environmental and experiential stresses is not at all good. A certain number, sheltered by some normal member of the family, maintain a colorless, uneventful existence while others become paupers, hoboes or petty criminals. The course of the hebephrenic form tends to be one of progressive deterioration although occasionally remissions occur before the final disorganization of personality. The question as to whether the paranoid type of schizophrenia ever recovers is sometimes raised. One's reply to this depends somewhat on a definition of terms. Undoubtedly remissions occur which may be looked upon as social recoveries. These intervals are rarely to be looked upon as ones of psychological recovery although during them the patient's adjustment may be well socialized and there be no distortions of reality in response to subjective needs. In general surly and bitter attitudes indicate a malignant process.

Finally, both for the sake of stating the opinion of one of the greatest students of schizophrenia as to the prognosis and for emphasizing the responsibility of the physician who undertakes the care of the early case of schizophrenia the conclusion of Bleuler must be quoted: "Although a certain number of patients become deteriorated with every treatment, and others improve even in apparently severe cases, the treatment will decide in more than one third of schizophrenic cases whether they can become social men again or not."

"Deterioration."—While schizophrenia may become arrested at any phase of its evolutionary course a word should be said about the nature of the unfavorable outcome so frequently observed. This malignant reaction was formerly spoken of as dementia. Such a characterization does not correctly indicate the personality change that may occur in schizophrenia. Dementia is an impersonal process, an impairment of intellectual function because of degeneration or destruction of neurones. Psychometric tests indicate that intellectual disturbances in schizophrenia are not similar to those in organic brain disease. In schizophrenia any apparent reduction in intelligence should be explained on the basis of emotional maladjustments. Long term psychologic studies of schizophrenic patients show that this apparent intellectual impairment is capable of recovery even after long periods of time. While there is no dementia in the strict sense of the word yet there is a reduction of, and subtle change in intellectual performance because of the long-continued influence on behavior of hallucinations, delusions, disorganizing fantasy states and the patient's autistic withdrawal into self. There is an impairment of contact between the patient and reality and of his ability to appreciate or respond to environmental demands. Reactions tend to become not merely unrelated but wholly irrelevant to the needs and purposes of normal adult life.

Perhaps the malignant state in which many cases terminate would better be described as a breaking up of personality organization, as a habit deterioration rather than as "mental deterioration," the term frequently applied. This malignant disorganization is not an invariable characteristic but is seen all too frequently on the "back wards" of mental hospitals. Here one finds the chronic schizophrenics, some sitting mutely on benches, others standing in a corner or pacing automatically to and fro, grimacing and absorbed in their delusions, bursting forth occasionally into spasms of hostility and aggression.

DIAGNOSIS

At times one observes perplexing similarities between schizophrenia and the minor psychoses or psychoneuroses, between schizophrenia and other biogenetic major psychoses, particularly manic-depressive, and rarely between it and organic mental disorders. It is doubtful if actually there is any definite demarcation between the psychoneurotic reaction and schizophrenia on the one hand and between the manic-depressive reaction and schizophrenia on the other. One will be exceedingly cautious in declaring that an isolated symptom is conclusive evidence of schizophrenia. In evaluating a symptom the clinical setting in which it occurs should be carefully examined. The eventual outcome should not, either, be the most important determinant in diagnosis.

Many of the differential points between schizophrenia and hysteria have been discussed in Chapter XXIII. In addition to what was then mentioned attention should be called to the fact that the onset in hysteria is usually more sudden and that a psychological motive is more apparent. In schizophrenic stupor one does not discover the expression of any emotional state. In hysterical stupor, on the other hand, one may note an expression of perplexity, fear, elation or of some other affective state. The history of an insidious change in interests points toward schizophrenia. Not only are the symptoms of hysteria more sudden in onset but they are more paroxysmal. The symptoms of hysteria are influenced more by certain persons in the environment. While the hysteric desires attention the schizophrenic is more apt to have periods when he is preoccupied, detached and apathetic. In schizophrenia the normal and psychotic elements exist side by side while in hysteria there is an alternation of normal and psychotic. The hysteric uses conventional, intelligible symbols while the schizophrenic uses individual or archaic ones. One can feel himself into the psychic life of the hysteric, but with difficulty, if at all, into that of the schizophrenic.

In the early stage of schizophrenia the differentiation from obsessive neurosis may be difficult. Sometimes schizophrenic reactions result from the release of primitive impulses that had previously been kept under control by the aid of obsessional symptoms. In schizophrenia there is usually more rumination and less tension than in the obsessive neurosis, the sufferer from which has a strong conscious resistance to his obsessions and compulsions, a resistance which is lacking in the schizophrenic since he is not particularly disturbed by them. Not rarely the schizophrenic in the early phases of the disorder expresses hypochondriacal complaints. His hypochondria lacks, however, the dramatization seen in the psychoneuroses.

Frequently one of the most difficult differentiations in mental disorders is between schizophrenia and manic-depressive psychosis. Doubtless this is in part, at least, due to the fact that many people are not pure schizoids or pure syntonics but rather are constitutional alloys and are characterized by admixtures in their personality. In addition to what has been said in the chapter on manic-depressive psychosis attention may be called to the fact that the onset of schizophrenia tends to be more insidious, that the excitement in schizophrenia is more frequently paroxysmal while that of the manic is more sustained and the mood of the schizophrenic rarely posesses the infectious quality seen in the manic-depressive. The delusions of the depressed schizophrenic are more grotesque than those of the depressed manic and he is less distressed by them. Illogical remarks and incongruous statements suggest schizophrenia. The difficulty in differentiating between these two disorders arises largely in the earlier stages of schizophrenia. With recurring episodes the schizophrenic nature of symptoms previously doubtful becomes more apparent with the result that confusion with manic-depressive symptomatology no longer exists. It very rarely happens that a psychosis apparently schizophrenic in its early phases proves subsequently to be of a manic-depressive reaction type. The reverse, however, is common.

There is usually no difficulty in distinguishing schizophrenia from epilepsy. Occasionally, nevertheless, the schizophrenic suffers from epileptiform or syncopal attacks which to the inexperienced observer strongly suggest the seizures of epilepsy. In that case one should inquire carefully as to whether the seizures or the mental symptoms appeared first, and should observe the nature of the seizure which in schizophrenia lacks the definiteness in type and the genuine disturbance of consciousness occurring in epilepsy. In epilepsy the most prominent symptom is the convulsion while in schizophrenia the seizure is a minor symptom, the disturbance in affect, in associations and the other schizophrenic features occupying the foreground.

In discussing the diagnosis of schizophrenia mention should be made of what is often spoken of as chronic alcoholic hallucinosis, attention to which is called not so much for pointing out distinctions from schizophrenia as for suggesting a possible identity with the latter disorder. The permanent persistence in the chronic alcoholic of auditory hallucinations in a setting of clear consciousness, frequently with systematized delusions was formerly considered as a symptom of an alcoholic psychosis. Many psychiatrists now believe that such cases are really schizophrenic reactions. In the discussion of the alcoholic psychoses attention was called to the fact that there is much to suggest that the so-called "acute" alcoholic hallucinosis has a schizophrenic basis and is not a purely alcoholic psychosis.

TREATMENT

As previously indicated it is undoubtedly true that disorders at the physiological or vegetative levels may disturb integration at the higher mental level of the organism. It is doubtful, however, if there is always an underlying disturbance at these lower levels in every case of schizophrenic reaction. At any rate it must be said that psychological conceptions are more helpful in enabling one to understand schizophrenia than are physiological and physicochemical. For the present, therefore, the preferred method of therapy must be to treat any demonstrable disturbances of organic processes, at the same time applying such psychological, social and physical measures as fit the situation and needs of the individual.

The treatment of schizophrenia, particularly in its early stages, is undertaken with far less pessimism than formerly. Its success depends to no small degree upon the therapeutic initiative, energy and effort of the physician, although the results will be small if the psychotic methods of thinking and feeling have become habits and established forms of adjustment.

Since it has been said that schizophrenia becomes manifest for the most part only after a prolonged period of incubation the question as to whether a disease so disorganizing to the personality cannot be prevented naturally arises. The goal of the modern mental hygiene movement with its child-guidance clinics and its school and college psychiatrists is not merely to prevent or correct faulty attitudes and the less malignant maladjustments of childhood or adolescence but to promote healthful patterns of feeling and thinking and to prevent the establishment of subterfuges and substitutions that result in imbalances of personality and finally culminate in the major psychoses of which schizophrenia is the most important. How far the rapidly growing mental hygiene movement will be able to modify the various factors the sequence of which leads to a schizophrenic adjustment to life is as yet entirely unknown and will probably never be susceptible of statistical demonstration. In the light of such knowledge as we now have, however, the body of principles included in the term mental hygiene seem to constitute the most rational means of preventing that malfunctioning of the personality known as schizophrenia. The shy, retiring, seclusive, unsociable child should receive careful psychotherapy designed to promote socialization and a wholesome adjustment between the growing personality and its environment.

After manifest schizophrenia has once developed, the success of treatment will vary directly with the stage of the disease in which it has been undertaken. A prolonged psychotic state tends in itself to develop or aggravate personality habit patterns of a deleterious nature. Gradually it is becoming appreciated that the most desirable time to treat schizophrenia is before the patient reaches the hospital for mental diseases, when he still possesses some insight, as many do early in the disease, when he still wants to be helped, when the conflicts and mechanisms, not yet concealed by a mass of superimposed symptoms, are comparatively undisguised, while the capacity of the emotional forces for readjusting themselves are still retained, and habits have not yet deteriorated. Every case must be studied and treated individually. Not only should the psychic level of the personality be examined for any factors which may be disturbing it but also the biochemical, physiological and neurological levels. Even though physiological or other somatic factors have apparently not acted as causal ones they should if possible be corrected. Unfortunately all too often the patient is not seen by the psychiatrist as early as desirable. Usually the patient should have been hospitalized long before the psychiatrist is consulted. The neutral environment provided by the hospital, the tolerant and understanding attitude of its personnel and the simple, orderly life may at once produce gratifying improvement.

Treatment will be directed toward two ends: by measures essentially mental in nature to discover and modify the factors and problems which have acted as disorganizing forces on the personality; second, to relieve special symptoms, particularly those that are troublesome or dangerous to the patient or disturbing to others. Constructive psychotherapy is limited unless the coöperation and confidence of the patient can be secured. Assisted by this rapport the physician seeks to understand the individual patient and his underlying strivings. One wishes therefore to learn the patient's mental content and the extent to which it is composed of fancies and projections. So far as possible his life experiences are learned and are then analyzed in the light of disturbing factors and the nature of the mental content. One watches for a common factor running through the patient's difficulties with himself and with others. Although the physician should recognize the dynamic relationship of factors, content and experiences to the patient's symptoms he will not interpret them to the patient. To be sure a cautious analysis of them sufficient to enable the patient gradually to discover their meaning is practicable in a limited number of schizophrenics. In this great care must be taken, particularly in the discussion of sensitive topics. If one goes beyond material which the patient can face safely fresh evidence of personality disorganization may appear. In only the early case of schizophrenia, and here in only a limited number of instances, will it be possible for the patient to recognize the meaning of his experiences and symptoms and to use this knowledge constructively in modifying his thinking and other personality functions.

Some psychiatrists believe that a modified psychoanalytic technique may at times be used successfully in the treatment of schizophrenia. Its use is limited since most schizophrenics, like many other psychotic patients, are incapable of developing therapeutically usable transference relationships with the psychiatrist.

As has been indicated one desires to have the patient acquire an objective attitude toward his beliefs and behavior—an attitude which he may use constructively in reorganizing his personality. The type of psychotherapy probably best adapted for this purpose is one in which by means of questions and problems submitted to him concerning past occurrences and reactions the patient is encouraged to investigate and study them for the factors involved. After this scrutiny he is guided in applying constructively to the task of correcting faulty tendencies and habits of thinking, the understanding which he has thus acquired. If the patient is psychotherapeutically inaccessible efforts should be directed toward re-education including the development of a wider social consciousness and the promotion of an interest in reality. One attempts to stimulate the patient's attention, detach his emotions from subjective material, redirect his interests to things outside of himself, inculcate healthful, socialized habits, and abstract him from his spiritual isolation. Among important aids to these ends are occupational therapy, games, music, and congenial companionships. Employment in some industry because it binds him more closely to reality has for years been known to be of great value to the introverted, preoccupied schizophrenic. Modern occupational therapy not only performs this purpose, but through the personal contact with the aide who often has some knowledge as to the psychopathology and needs of the schizophrenic it frequently adds the agency of that personal emotional relationship known as the transference in redirecting interest. Its techniques should be those that will aid in socialization. While not a few patients become permanently isolated in their own autistic lives in spite of every effort at treatment yet the degree of improvement is, broadly speaking, directly proportional to the attention and treatment that they receive. There is usually a tendency to a progressive introversion and habit-deterioration. A constant effort should therefore be made to maintain or reëstablish an affective contact with reality and prevent the patient from drifting into a state of inactivity and indifference. The patient should be encouraged in occupation and his environment should provide as many as possible of those things of life that interest and satisfy the person in mental health. Music, dancing, moving pictures, dramatics, baseball and other games and recreational activities all have a useful place. The hospital offers a protective environment adapted to the patient's capacity for adjustment. Its treatment should undoubtedly be socialized to a greater extent than is now the case. In no instance should the patient be lost in the obscurity of a chronic ward. It has been said that the picture one sees in chronic and hopeless institutional cases is one third due to disease, while two thirds is a reaction to an unfavorable and unsuitable environment. Institutions are now adopting a more active and aggressive policy of treatment but are handicapped in their efforts because they do not receive the patient sufficiently early in the course of his disease and because they do not have sufficient personnel to render available the known resources of treatment. One of the unfortunate conditions that still exists widely in public institutions is overcrowding which results in a lack of adequate attention, provides an unnatural environment and promotes neglect, abuses, injuries, and confusion. In the ideal institution the hospital would provide what the home cannot, in addition to the advantages which the patient would have received had he remained in the home.

In 1939 Myerson described what he termed the "total push" method for the treatment of the institutionalized chronic schizophrenic. This did not involve any new principles of treatment but consists of the sustained application of an organized program of diversified and individual activities designed to prevent or relieve the schizophrenic deterioration undoubtedly often aggravated by the psychologic vacuum of the "back ward." Measures which tend to arouse the patient from his automatized isolation are vigorously employed day by day. An attempt is made not to emphasize the separation created by the patient's illness, but to create as nearly as possible an atmosphere like the general community. Daily, weather permitting, the patient is taken for walks. Sustained, active efforts are made to overcome the inertia of the patient and his resistance to participation in games and exercise. Classes in bowling are organized and a game room is provided. As patients improve they participate in dancing, music, craftsmanship and general occupational therapy. Physiotherapeutic measures such as showers, douches and massage are utilized daily. Diet is liberal and small doses of insulin are often employed. Stress is placed on keeping the patient properly dressed in attractive clothing. The patient is shaved regularly and fingers and hair receive careful attention. Praise in the presence of the group and reward under the same circumstances are liberally utilized as motives. The relationships developed between patient and the worker are of therapeutic value. The participation of the employees in these highly organized activities improves their morale and promotes a greater interest in the welfare of the patient.

There are numerous special symptoms that may require treatment. Catatonic excitement is best treated by the continuous bath. Occasionally a patient because of restlessness will not remain in the bath, in which case wet packs may be employed. Restraint and seclusion promote neglect and abuse and provoke fear, distrust, suspicion and resentment in the mind of the patient, and prevent or destroy that rapport between patient on the one hand and physician and nurses on the other so essential to any successful therapy. Sedative drugs may be used to promote sleep or allay excitement but their use should be carefully guarded lest they be employed too frequently and in too large amounts. The various barbituric acid derivatives are among the most useful, although paraldehyde, bromides and chloral may be employed in moderation. Many, perhaps most, institutions for mental diseases use sedative drugs exceedingly sparingly because of the abuse of them that may easily arise. Narcotics should never be used. In catatonic stupor note should be made as to whether bowels and bladder are emptied. Not rarely the stuporous patient fails to eat. If persuasive efforts are not successful spoon feeding should be tried. Finally if the patient shows definite signs of malnutrition or acetone appears in the urine one must resort to tube feeding. Instructions concerning the content of a suitable feeding mixture and as to the procedure of nasal tube feeding will be found on pages 347–348.

Special Forms of Treatment

Insulin Therapy.—The history of the therapy of schizophrenia has been characterized by the use of various forms which temporarily had enthusiastic proponents but failed to stand the test of time. Although insulin therapy is not a specific and has in many respects been a disappointing procedure yet when given at the right time to the right kind of case it is probably the most effective form of therapy now available. The manner by which it produces beneficial results is unknown but it is probably through modification of the carbohydrate metabolism of the cortical cell and of the central nervous system as a whole. The percentage of complete remissions following insulin therapy depends largely on the previous duration of the psychosis. The recovery rate is by far the greatest in patients who have not been ill for more than six months. Full remission in patients who have been ill more than two years is not common. Recovery after illness of longer duration is not rare if there have been symptom-free periods during the illness. The variations in reports of results secured by insulin therapy are probably due to several factors. Some psychiatrists require full insight as the only satisfactory evidence of full recovery. Others consider that the persistence of slight personality changes is not inconsistent with recovery. Reports of low recovery rates have often been made by psychiatrists who failed to apply as long and as deep comas as those who have reported greater success. Often, too, they did not continue treatments over as long a period as did the more successful. Best results seem to be secured by physicians who closely followed the technique recommended by Sakel. Many psychiatrists believe that in cases of less then one year's duration adequate treatment is followed by immediate improvement more frequently than is any other form of therapy. The percentage of relapses is high—so high that some psychiatrists believe that after a period of five years the percentage of patients who have remained well is no greater than those whose remissions were spontaneous. Bond and Rivers found that at the end of treatment 55 per cent of all patients treated were enjoying a remission, after one year of treatment 42 per cent continued the remission, after two years 36 per cent were recovered or in a remission, while after three years 32 per cent had maintained their favorable condition. Other writers report that only one fourth to one third of the successfully treated cases maintain their remission after three to four and a half years. The best results are secured in those patients in whom the prognosis would, in general, be most favorable, *i.e.*, in cases characterized by acute onset, acute symptomatology, exogenic precipitating factors, catatonic reaction and previous extraversive tendencies. It is usually agreed that insulin therapy not only increases the number of remissions but also improves their quality as compared to spontaneous remissions. Not only is the length of the patient's residence in a hospital reduced by insulin therapy but more patients can thereby be returned to the community through its use. Combined insulin and electroconvulsive therapy may succeed where the two treatments given separately have failed. Insulin therapy in paranoid forms produces better results than in hebephrenic or simple types. Treatment is not followed by any change in the prepsychotic personality.

Electric Convulsive Therapy.—Because of the simplicity of its application, because of its fewer hazards and because specially trained personnel need not be as large there is now a tendency to substitute electric convulsive for insulin therapy. There continues to be some controversy as to the relative results secured by these two forms of therapy. It would seem probable that a slightly larger number of full remissions will be secured by insulin therapy yet many psychiatrists believe that if electric shock treatment is prolonged and intensive with at least 20 treatments it is as effective as insulin. The results are better if the symptoms are acute and florid and if affective features are present. Patients who relapse after each of two successive courses of treatment may be kept on a maintenance treatment regimen of one or two treatments a week. The care and supervision of problem, chronically disturbed schizophrenics is also much facilitated by a similar maintenance course. Great caution should be exercised, however, in prolonging maintenance treatment. In not a few cases patients who have received many treatments develop "spontaneous" convulsions possessing the characteristics of epilepsy and continue to follow the course of that disease after discontinuance of treatments. In some cases spontaneous seizures have occurred after 48 treatments. In other cases seizures first appeared after 150 or more treatments.

Combined Insulin-Convulsive Treatment.—Since neither insulin nor electric convulsive therapy is always effective a combination of the two forms may be more satisfactory. Electric convulsive therapy may be utilized on insulin-free days or, perhaps preferably, convulsions may be induced electrically at the time of the deepest hypoglycemic coma. Because convulsive therapy is simpler in application and quicker in results many psychiatrists begin treatment with convulsive therapy followed by insulin treatment to stabilize the improvement. If a schizophrenic patient fails to improve under one method various combinations of treatment may be tried. (See also Chapter XXX.)

Prefrontal Lobotomy.—This form of treatment will not be employed except as a last resort but if it is to be employed it should be used before emotional deterioration is well advanced. If after one year of active treatment which has included a full course of insulin therapy, electric shock, and combined insulin and electric shock therapies the patient has shown no improvement frontal lobotomy is to be recommended. Best results are secured if the patient's original personality was relatively well organized. Patients who are chronically excited, tense, resistive, destructive or combative are suitable subjects for lobotomy. The problem of their care is usually much simplified in the case of those who do not improve sufficiently to permit discharge from a hospital. As Freeman states, while a schizophrenic is still fighting his disease prefrontal lobotomy offers a chance for relief and for consequent improvement in behavior. Results in patients who have been hospitalized for as long as ten or twelve years are usually unsatisfactory. (See also pp. 473–474.)

BIBLIOGRAPHY

Association for Research in Nervous and Mental Disease: Vol. V, Schizophrenia (Dementia Praecox). New York, Paul B. Hoeber, Inc., 1928.

———: Vol. X, Schizophrenia (Dementia Praecox). Baltimore, Williams and Wilkins Co., 1931.

Bender, Lauretta: Childhood Schizophrenia. Am. J. Orthopsychiat., *17:* 40, 1947.

Blair, Donald: Prognosis in Schizophrenia. J. Ment. Sc., *86:* 378–477, 1940.

Bleuler, E.: Dementia Praecox oder Gruppe der Schizophrenien. In Aschaffenburg's Handbuch der Psychiatrie. Bd. 2. Leipzig, Franz Deuticke, 1911.

———: The Theory of Schizophrenic Negativism. Translated by W. A. White. J. Nerv. & Ment. Dis., *39:* 50, 133, 274, 1912.

———: Textbook of Psychiatry. Translated by A. A. Brill. New York, Macmillan, 1924.

———: Primäre und sekundäre Symptome der Schizophrenie. Ztschr. f. d. ges. Neurol. u. Psychiat., *124:* 607, 1930.

———: The Physiogenic and Psychogenic in Schizophrenia. Am. J. Psychiat., *10:* 203, 1930.

SCHIZOPHRENIA (DEMENTIA PRAECOX)

Bleuler, M.: Schizophrenia: Review of Work of Prof. Eugen Bleuler. Arch. Neurol. and Psychiat., *26:* 610, 1931.

Bond, E. D., and Shurley, J. T.: Insulin Therapy and its Future. Am. J. Psychiat., *103:* 338, 1946.

Bond, E. D., and Rivers, T. D.: Insulin Shock Therapy after Seven Years. Am. J. Psychiat., *101:* 62, 1944.

Bradley, Chas.: Schizophrenia in Childhood. New York, The Macmillan Company, 1941.

Campbell, C. M.: Toward Mental Health. Cambridge, Harvard Univ. Press, 1933.

———: Destiny and Disease in Mental Disorders. New York, W. W. Norton & Co., 1935.

———: Clinical Studies in Schizophrenia. Am. J. Psychiat., *99:* 475, 1943.

———: Adolf Meyer. Arch. Neurol. & Psychiat., *37:* 715, 1937.

Cheney, C. O., and Drewry, P. H. Jr.: Results of Non-Specific Treatment in Dementia Praecox. Am. J. Psychiat., *95:* 203-217, 1938.

Folks, Homer, *et al:* Insulin Shock Therapy; Study by the Temporary Commission on State Hospital Problems. New York, 1944.

Freeman, W., and Watts, J. W.: Prefrontal Lobotomy. The Problem of Schizophrenia. Am. J. Psychiat., *101:* 739, 1945.

Hanfmann, E., and Kasanin, J.: Conceptual Thinking in Schizophrenia. New York, Nervous and Mental Disease Monographs, 1943.

Hecker, Ewald: Die Hebephrenie. Berlin, Virchow's Archiv, 1871.

Himwich, H. E., *et al.:* Biochemical Changes Occurring in the Cerebral Blood During the Insulin Treatment of Schizophrenia. J. Nerv. & Ment. Dis., *89:* 273, 1939.

Hoch, August: Constitutional Factors in the Dementia Praecox Group. Rev. Neurol. and Psychiat., *8:* 463, 1910.

Hoskins, R. G.: The Biology of Schizophrenia. New York, W. W. Norton & Co., 1946.

Jung, C. G.: Psychology of Dementia Praecox. Translated by Peterson and Brill. Washington, Nervous and Mental Disease Publishing Co., 1909.

———: Psychological Types. New York, Harcourt, Brace & Co., 1923.

———: On the Psychogenesis of Schizophrenia. J. Ment. Sc., *85:* 999, 1939.

Kahlbaum, Karl: Die Katatonie oder das Spannungsirresein. Berlin, August Hirschwald, 1874.

Kalinowsky, L. B., and Hoch, P. H.: Shock Treatments. New York, Grune & Stratton, 1946.

Kallman, F. J.: The Genetic Theory of Schizophrenia. Am. J. Psychiat., *103:* 309, 1946.

Kallman, F. J., *et al.*: The Rôle of Mental Deficiency in the Incidence of Schizophrenia. Am. J. Ment. Deficiency, *45:* 514, 1941.

Kasanin, J.: Language and Thought in Schizophrenia. Berkeley, Univ. of California Press, 1944.

Katzenelbogen, S.: Dementia Praecox, Formulation by Kraepelin, Bleuler and Meyer Psychiatric Quart., *16:* 439, 1942.

———: A Critical Appraisal of the "Shock Therapies" in the Major Psychoses, I—Insulin. Psychiatry, *2:* 493, 1939; *3:* 211, 1940; *3:* 409, 1940.

Knight, R. P.: Psychotherapy of an Adolescent Catatonic Schizophrenic with Mutism. Psychiatry, *9:* 323, 1946.

Kraepelin, E.: Dementia Praecox. Translated by Barclay, E., and S. Livingstone, Edinburgh, 1919.

Kretschmer, E.: Physique and Character. New York, Harcourt, Brace & Co., 1925.

Lewis, N. D. C.: The Constitutional Factors in Dementia Praecox. Washington, Nervous and Mental Disease Publishing Co., 1923.

———: Research in Dementia Praecox. New York, The National Committee for Mental Hygiene, 1936.

Lowrie, R. S., *et al:* Studies on the Prognosis in Schizophrenic-Like Psychoses in Children. Am. J. Psychiat., *99:* 542, 1943.

May, James V.: The Dementia Praecox-Schizophrenia Problem. Am. J. Psychiat., *11:* 401, 1931.

Mayer-Gross, W., and Moore, N. P.: Schizophrenia. Recent Progress in Psychiatry. Ed. by G. W. T. H. Fleming. London, J. & A. Churchill, 1944.

Meyer, Adolf: An Attempt at Analysis of the Neurotic Constitution. Jour. Abnormal Psychol., *14:* 90, 1903.

———: Fundamental Conceptions of Dementia Praecox. Brit. Med. Jour., Part 2, 757, 1906; J. Nerv. and Ment. Dis., *34:* 331, 1907.

———: Dynamic Interpretation of Dementia Praecox. Am. J. Psychol., *21:* 385, 1910.

———: The Nature and Conception of Dementia Praecox. Jour. Abnormal Psychol., 5: 274, 1910.

———: Constructive Formulation of Schizophrenia. Am. J. Psychiat., *78:* 355, 1922.

Morel, B. A.: Traité des Maladies Mentales. Paris, Victor Masson, 1860.

Myerson, A.: Theory and Principles of the "Total Push" Method in the Treatment of Chronic Schizophrenia. Am. J. Psychiat., *95:* 1197, 1939.

Rennie, T. A. C.: Analysis of One Hundred Cases of Schizophrenia with Recovery. Arch. Neurol. and Psychiat., *46:* 197, 1941.

Sakel, M.: Pharmacological Shock Treatment of Schizophrenia. Washington, Nervous and Mental Disease Publishing Co., 1938.

Sargant, W., and Slater, E.: An Introduction to Somatic Methods of Treatment in Psychiatry. Baltimore, Williams & Wilkins Co., 1944.

Dementia Praecox (Schizophrenia)

Dementia Praecox (early Dementia) or Schizophrenia (Split Mind)

THIS disease is more obscure, as far as origin and symptoms are concerned, than any other form of mental disturbance. Prof. Kraepelin of Munich named it Dementia Praecox, a name which indicates two important conditions of the disease. The first is that it occurs early in life; the second that it results in grave, permanent disturbance of all mental faculties.

As the disease may originate at any age and does not nearly always result in dementia, this term was considered less appropriate. In more recent years, Prof. Bleuler of Zurich named it Schizophrenia, meaning split mind. He considered the fundamental condition of this disease to exist in splitting of the personality. This term, superficially considered, has much in its favor as in this disease the unity and harmony of all mental activities and functions is, often for a shorter or longer period, seriously disturbed. It is my belief, however, that there is no evidence to prove a disturbance deeper than physiological processes. The personality, I am convinced, is a unit and not open to splitting or division.

Over 18% of admissions belong to this group. Of mental hospital population, 65% are schizophenics.

The cause is obscure, but in many, hereditary factors are found.

The type of individual most frequently affected is the unsociable, shut-in type. Temperamentally, he may be either cold or sensitive, both qualities tending to isolation. Either society shuns him or he recoils from society.

Vague forebodings of gloom are often an early symptom of its insidious onset. The patient begins to complain of being tired and sits around staring, absorbed in his thoughts. If urged to work, he is irritable or becomes emotional. He laughs and cries without cause and may show no affection to those he formerly loved. Sleep is nearly always badly disturbed, but sleeplessness not complained of. Hallucinations of all senses are very common and often of an unpleasant, gruesome nature.

The almost numberless varieties into which this disease has been divided Kraepelin organized into four main groups, and authorities in general have followed his classification.

The four outstanding types are: simple, hebephrenic, katatonic, and paranoid.

THE FOUR OUTSTANDING TYPES:

1. Simple

This condition is characterized by a destruction of the whole psychic life and a course of events, so gradual, that even those of the patient's own household do not know when the disease set in.

The symptoms are about as follows: They begin to fail in school or other pursuits in which they were formerly successful. In early stages of the disease, the sufferer may make desperate attempts to regain his former initiative and ability to succeed. All attempts to overcome the crushing effect of the malady are, however, futile. The course of the disease is at times intermittent. Slowly there may be a partial restoration to normal mental functioning, but often the symptoms recur, making ever deeper inroads.

More advanced cases are emotional, irritable, indolent, and obstinate. The sympathy for others and attachment to the ones they previously loved, becomes dulled. Affection for parents changes to complete indifference or positive antagonism. The latter can probably often be explained as due to unkind treatment. They are misunderstood and their symptoms misinterpreted. For this reason they are scolded, threatened, and punished. They are accused of bringing the condition upon themselves by an immoral life. Masturbation, drinking, smoking, and the harboring of evil thoughts are especially considered the cause of patients' unusual reactions.

The final picture of these cases after years of suffering is one of complete indifference. There is no goal or purpose in life. The attachment to place and person vanishes. The tramp, beggar, alms house inmate, and prostitute, are often examples of its ravages.

2. Hebephrenic (Insanity of youth)

It is similar to the simple dementia, and may appear as the final stage of that condition. Its onset is usually more acute and severe, however, and among the outstanding symptoms are hallucinations of all the senses and a strong delusional content.

The early symptoms are rather frequently a marked depressive episode, with religious or strong suicidal inclinations. It may also be ushered in by a period of extreme confusion. After the initial symptoms, the disease, if recovery does not ensue, follows a rather regular course.

The patient slowly secludes himself and if possible remains in bed entirely covered by blankets. He is disinterested in his surroundings, and love for relatives and former friends disappears. If not allowed to remain in bed, he seeks some secluded corner and sits there, often in the most awkward position. Outbursts of causeless, silly laughter, and weeping are common. If not molested the patients usually seem fairly well at ease, but if urged to change their position or to perform some duty, they become irritable and may fly into a rage. If they are willing to write, it will be noticed that the stream of thought has become irrelevant and incoherent.

The final picture is a condition of extreme deterioration, both physical and mental.

3. Katatonic

As in the case of the hebephrenic types, the condition is often ushered in by a period of depression. The onset is, however, more sudden, and the early symptoms more suggestive of mental disease.

Many cases rather suddenly become confused and wander from home or take the train to some distant city. In this state they resemble the hysterical amnesias, but are, in contra-distinction to the hysterical fugeus, liable to become violent if restrained or urged to return.

In this katatonic condition, there is a strong and terrifying hallucinatory and delusional content. The period of excitement which may last from weeks to months, is followed by a condition of stupor. During this time, all voluntary movements cease, they neither walk, speak, nor eat. The thought processes are blocked, the muscles go into a state of waxy flexibility during which the extremities can be placed in any abnormal position and will stay there till changed (catalepsy).

The condition stands open to change, both emotional and physical. There are outbursts of sudden irritability and violence. A mute, negativistic, stuporous patient may suddenly run, jump, strike, kick or scream. One of our patients, quietly standing behind a 30-foot high building, suddenly ran as a human fly up the back of this building, and after arriving at the top, jumped down on an ash pile. Unharmed, he stood for a minute, then made a break for liberty, only to stop mute as suddenly as he had begun his dangerous ascent.

A typical case of katatonic dementia praecox does not evidence the extreme deterioration of the first two types. Behind that apparently inpenetrable wall, the mental functions often remain fairly well preserved. I have seen these patients, after six years of extreme stupor, respond fairly well for short periods, both emotionally and intellectually.

4. Paranoid

This condition is as insidious as the simple form, but occurs late in life and may be secondary to the other types. It differs from pure paranoia and paranoid conditions in that it results in deterioration and has no systematized delusions.

After some 5 years, during which the symptoms are obscure and only recognized by those of their own household, the disease assumes more outstanding and dangerous proportions. The early symptoms of suspicion, ideas of reference, and persecution are intensified. The patient becomes irritable and threatening and seeks aid from governmental authorities against the imagined persecutors. Finally, outburst of rage, resulting from dreadful hallucinations, may drive the sufferer to acts of violence.

After this date, the course is usually variable. There may be weeks of calm and contentment, but these periods are often followed by days of extreme mental and emotional storm. A certain number become satisfied to live in a self-centered delusional world. One said to me, "If they call this crazy, I am entirely satisfied to remain this way." But there are others in whom for years and decades the delusional content periodically disturbs the patient.

DEMENTIA PRAECOX (SCHIZOPHRENIA)

ALL GROUPS:

All types have a rather serious prognosis or outcome. After the first acute attack, there is usually a temporary recovery. In some 20 per cent of the katatonic, the patient's recovery is permanent.

As the attacks follow each other in a more or less rapid succession, the sufferer slowly deteriorates. This deterioration may show itself as years pass, both physically and mentally. The memory is, contrary to the impression left by the patient, not disturbed. He pays no attention to visitors and is not at all interested in his environment. The affective life is in many almost entirely destroyed. The paranoid type bears up best under the disease, and may even after years show very little change.

Treatment, in most cases, demands institutional care and protection to prevent suicide, homicide, etc. Isolation is dangerous. The patient should be kept, as far as conditions permit, in contact with the outside world and reality. The care of these patients during the early stage often demands the utmost tact, patience, and firmness. Graded work, after rest, should be encouraged. They must never be locked up alone, but should be kept with other patients. The presence of other mental cases, even if badly deteriorated, has a valuable restraining influence.

The shock treatment, produced by insulin, metrazol, etc., may give a new hope in the treatment of early cases of this dreadful disease.

Schizoid: Hebephrenic Form (Case 13)

(a) *Hospital stay*: 15 years.

(b) *Duration* of acute psychosis: 5 years.

(c) *Outcome*: Marked deterioration.

She was a well-developed, quiet country girl, who a year before admission had become afflicted with a sense of heaviness and apprehension. More recently this depressed feeling became interrupted with short periods of silly laughter and an attitude of complete indifference. The periods of gloom of late had become more marked and a fear of death overwhelmed her. Palpitation of the heart and other strange bodily sensations increased her anxiety by day and unpleasant dreams terrorized her at night. Everything imaginable was tried to obtain relief, but of no avail. It is true, there were periods of remission, but these were usually short, and invariably followed by new attacks of greater severity than the preceding.

A longing for death to escape this unhappy existence tormented her. As by a mysterious hand, she was at times drawn to the quiet waters of a nearby lake. But life was still too dear, and suicide for her spelled eternal doom.

When questioned concerning her emotional life, she answered, "I feel awful. I cannot express it. I am afraid of everybody and nobody in particular. I fear death, but at times I wish to die. I may, however, not take my own life."

The last three months she spent at home, she sat for hours in one position, staring into space. If urged to work, she showed signs of irritability and at times became violent. Her nights were often sleepless and spent in roaming through the house, while during the day she frequently kept to bed, refusing to dress and assist with work. Attention to self and bodily needs were neglected. Although previously she was a model as concerned dress and general toilet, she was now indifferent. The food she ate was gulped down in haste and not obtained at the family board, but taken direct from the pantry and cupboard.

A letter written to her mother shortly after entering our hospital, gives insight into her mental content. The fact that this girl was reared in a home burdened by mystical religious tendencies, increases the picture of despondency from which she suffered, but on the whole the letter is a striking example of early depression found in many types of mental disturbance:

"I live," she wrote, "in a morbid state of mind, and to obtain relief from this I am writing you. An unexplainable obsession controls me, suggesting that I may not live, and a feeling of guilt because of my sins overpowers me. I scarcely dare speak to others. My conscience does not allow me. Just what the origin of these thoughts is, is a mystery to me. Whether God causes them to enter my mind, or the devil, I know not. I even fear to eat and I am not worthy to occupy the ground upon which I stand. The thought that is ever with me, is that I am lost. I scarcely dare to touch the Bible with my hands because I am sinful, but I do not dare to put it aside because of the judgment day. Whether God causes these thoughts to originate in my mind or whether my *weak nervous system* is at the root of the trouble, is not clear to me. At times I work desperately hard believing it to be my duty. But even this irritates me because I am convinced that work will not bring salvation. The words 'Not to the strong is the battle, nor to the swift is the race, but to the true and the faithful, victory is promised by Grace,' are ever with me. There are nights that I think I may not sleep and that I am not worthy to have a bed to rest on. But in turn my mind replies, 'It is within the providence of God that I was born, and for this reason he wants me to live and keep well," for "Not a hair can fall from our head without God's will.' The thought that I have sinned against you and the nurses also obsesses me, but this does not harmonize with the teaching that 'man can sin only against God.' It also occurs to me that I may not desire to be near you, mother, as you have also suffered agony of soul, but I believe mother is one of the elect. I do not dare express my feeling to the nurses as I consider myself too worthless. I do not feel this way the entire day, but nearly so.

"Your loving daughter."

This letter reveals little as to the seriousness of the mental disease from which she is suffering. There still is perfect logic in her thought processes. Her moods, although swinging between rather wide extremes may be within the range of normal, and the affective or love life expressed in her desire to be with dear ones, is entirely normal. The general course of the condition, however, points to the possible presence of a malignant mental disease, a disease which if it continues long or is severe, causes irreparable damage to the personality.

In order to prove to you that this patient really was suffering from symptoms of early mental disturbance, let me read to you parts of two letters written respectively three and six years after the above.

Three years have elapsed. She still stares into space, is indolent, indifferent about her appearance, and at times irritable and moody. A grave change has, however, occurred in her mental life, as the following incoherent letter illustrates:

"Dear Friend:

"I am all set for a little fight in the best of time. It will be saved for them because then it is going to be all saved at the same time and it got fun on earth because it got most of fun with her baby darling again. It is better again it is too sad.

"Yours truly."

Another three years passed by, more stormy than the former. She has at times been violent, was always very confused and entirely indifferent as to her appearance. A note written at this time clearly illustrates all absence of logical thought sequence. Only disconnected words seem to fill her consciousness.

She wrote:

"candy candy Louis nervous letter jumped kind Miss candy lap no more Miss Massachusetts no more. Ida Clara Clara Ida I laughed I can't to write."

The final picture of this patient after an affliction of fifteen years can be best obtained from the monthly nurses' report: "Patient was dressed at 7 A.M. Fairly good-natured, but has irritable spells. At times troublesome and very restless [she will run about as if chased] but is usually silent, dull, indolent, contrary and resistive."

Hope for recovery in this patient is absent. She has undergone considerable deterioration and will never again fully appreciate social and religious values. But since the memory content is not affected, she may after the inward storm subsides, adjust herself fairly well in a protected environment, and to a degree find comfort and solace in the faith she once professed.

Schizoid: Hebephrenic, Katatonic mixture

(Case 14)

(a) *Duration* of Condition: 2 years.

(b) *Outcome*: Social Adjustment.

***Extracts from letters*:**

"I hope you are feeling fine, 'cause health means so much more than all the riches of this world.' I feel like I just lost completely everything, but will pray to our

Heavenly Father, who with his infinite love looks down upon His people. [She does her utmost to cling to her faith.] 'Whom have I Lord in heaven but Thee?' I can't remember the rest. I can't write much. It tires me too much. You'll have to excuse me. [The feeling of tiredness is often extreme in this type of mental derangement. It borders on exhaustion and is interpreted by the patient as a symptom of sickness.] I can hardly write. Can't sleep, can't eat.

"These voices [hallucinations] tell me everything I hear; I mean when anybody speaks to me, when they say nasty things [hallucinations frequently include thoughts relating to the reproductive functions.] It is getting worse all the time. When I write it makes me cry; also when I talk. [emotional instability] I never before [evidently refers to day-dreaming] saw things in my mind like I do now [hallucinations].

"I don't think there's any use in trying to get better because it seems like all my aunts and uncles and also the doctors that helped me are speaking to me. It's funny, but it's true. And that's what keeps going round and round in circles.

"When another patient hollers the same thing goes through my mind and the same holds true when anyone talks to me. When I read letters their contents seem to be repeated in my head. When I move I can see myself move. When I go downstairs I can see myself upstairs, just can see myself being moved constantly."

[The whole represents a hyper-sensitive sensory and memory mechanism. Any wave set in action is repeated manifold. These waves may be set in motion by external forces as in reading, listening, movement, etc., or may originate in the memory sphere.

It is therefore rather important to keep such individuals in an environment that is unchanging, but they should never be allowed to be alone with their delusions and hallucinations.]

DEMENTIA PRAECOX (SCHIZOPHRENIA)

Schizoid: Katatonic Form. (Case 15)

(a) *Hospital stay*: 6 months.

(b) *Duration* of active disease: 4 months.

(c) *Outcome*: Mild deterioration (social recovery).

The patient was one of a family of nine. The grandfather died senile; an aunt was at one time mentally deranged, but the family in general was well-balanced, healthy, and thrifty.

Physically, he had always enjoyed unusually good health, but for the last few months complained of headache, dizziness and blurring of vision.

Socially, he stood aloof, but was regular in the attendance of meetings, both secular and religious. For the opposite sex he felt little attraction, in fact, soon was bored in the presence of women.

The past summer his relatives had observed a marked change in his views and habits. Whereas previously he had attended only the local church, he now began to neglect this church, and to frequent revival meetings. He also expressed unusual trends of thought. He said, "I receive visions from God urging me to become a missionary." A letter written at that time well illustrates these early symptoms. He wrote: "I desire to write father a letter to inform you that I am not busy with manual work, but desire to study the Bible, the Book. I study this to obtain wisdom of God and to gain strength and courage to preach woe to mankind." Shortly after writing this missive, he exhibited intense fear. He said, "The government is on my track and I will soon be put to death." He cried and prayed for hours, hid in the house and sought protection by police and church authorities. Food he refused, believing it to be poisoned, and his sleep was greatly disturbed.

In this condition of panic he entered the hospital, where during the first few days he showed marked improvement. The protection of closed doors apparently calmed his fearful mind and the presence of strangers stimulated him to control his delusional thoughts. This improvement, however, was of short duration. After a few days he sank into a deep stupor. This stupor was associated with rigidity of all muscles, and complete blocking of thought. He would stand speechless for hours in one and the same position. These periods of katatonic stupor were interspersed with occasional impulsive acts like striking, running, turning somersaults, screaming, etc.

Food he finally refused and had to be fed by tube. His bodily needs he ignored and was cared for as an infant during its first months of life.

After two months, this period of stupor, negativism, impulsive episodes, and irritability slowly cleared up. His confusion and fear subsided, he regained interest in his environment and work, and soon was able to return home.

His recovery was, however, not complete. The personality was warped. His affective or love life, his religious ideals, and altruistic desires were no longer as before the sickness. This lack came out clearly in a letter written to me sometime after his return home. After telling of his trip home and present activities, he ended the letter by expressing a desire to amass wealth. No word was written about relatives or friends, no greetings left to nurses who had cared for him, and not a single word expressing a desire that our work might prosper.

His life had become self-centered and devoid of warmth. Natural love for relatives had lessened, religious ideals became stagnant and altruistic motives vanished.

We have here the history of a healthy, energetic, reliable, conscientious young man, who, without evident reason, becomes afflicted with mental disease, passes through an acute, severe period of mental panic and recovers, but loses essential human traits.

What will be his future? Most cases of this type live a fairly well adjusted social life. In many there is, however, lack of contact. They live alone. Marriage they shun. Religious observance, if not entirely neglected, is no more than a routine. Interest on the whole is limited to physical animal needs. The tramp population and prostitute group find many in their camps that at one time suffered from this type of mental disease.

The seriousness of this type of mental disturbance is not to be sought in symptoms this disease may produce, but in the deteriorating effect on the organism. Some escape entirely unscathed, others, like our patient, show greater or smaller character deviations, and again others must be institutionalized the rest of their days.

Schizoid: Paranoid type (Case 16)

Extracts from letters.
Normal parts:

"Dear mother: I hear you are not feeling so well nowadays. I hope you will soon feel much better. Are the children much trouble to you? I would so love to care for them myself."

Delusional parts:

After asking some questions concerning their family history, she continues: "I know those questions sound funny, but there is a terrible funny sickness going around nowadays—radio sickness, they call it, and scientists are puzzling over it. I believe that radio is not as new as people have believed, but that some person who for years used it is becoming incautious because he thinks he is unconquerable. I believe my trouble was caused by the radio. I have found the names of mechanisms and what they do in the dictionary. I believe that somebody is so dead against the Christians that he or they are concentrating on them.

"That radio wave made me faint and gave me the notion I was being poisoned, and then because I was afraid of poison I did not dare to eat much, which made me weak and unable to do my work or think clearly. Then I heard voices, and I'm sure it came because of the radio. Then I was afraid to sleep. They gave me sleeping tablets and being weakened by lack of food, I talked a whole day feverishly and suffered from delirium. I still hear voices which I know by this time come from some radio machinery. I was just conscious enough last summer to realize that they were adjusting wires on some of the buildings here so they could keep me hearing voices and other patients, too, no doubt.

"One of these voices insisted that I commit suicide to rid my congregation of an incompetent. Why they were after me I do not know, but perhaps they are after my money. They say the most terrible things and show a person the most awful pictures, but I have found words in one of the latest dictionaries showing that there are machines that do such things.

"If you ever hear voices, don't worry and don't be afraid to eat. The radio waves tasted rather funny, coppery like, but it is not poison. A person needs a lawyer or detective rather than a doctor, seems to me.

"I at first suspected the doctor, but everything is so nice here and everybody so kind and considerate, that I began to think about it, and some of my thoughts are hard to explain, but due to the articles I find in the paper I believe I am on the right track. Some scientist, one or more, has gone mad with his invention, and is behind it all."

Schizoid: Paranoid type (Case 17)

(a) *Duration*: Some 5 years.

(b) Personality well preserved. No signs of deterioration.

DEMENTIA PRAECOX (SCHIZOPHRENIA)

"I mistrusted my husband. I can't prove anything against him, but I know.

"I am not under any strain. I am just as healthy as any one. I just should not listen to whispers I heard for a year. People can talk with their eyes. Thoughts are transferred from eyes. I thought long ago that I heard God's voice. I am sure I did. It happened about 3 to 4 years ago in the night. The devil does not talk much to me. Just before I left home, it was all microphones about the house. If I had a gun I would show the people who trouble me."

Patient at home periodically scolded and raved for hours; at other periods she was pleasant, clear, and sorry for attacks of violence.

The first few weeks at the hospital she was greatly relieved. The new impressions evidently ruled out the hallucinations, but before a month had passed, she wrote me a note stating:

"Dear Doctor:

"Will you please write to my husband and tell him I've got the same *terrible* problems here as what happens at home. She [the imagined persecutor] just keeps on concentrating on me, and hurting my head all the time. Please write my husband and tell him to take me farther away from home."

DEMENTIA PRÆCOX

§ 1. Nature of the Disorder.

DEMENTIA PRÆCOX is a term applied to a variety of signs and symptoms which occur chiefly in adolescents, but which cannot yet be said to describe a definite disease entity. Kraepelin, who has done most of recent years to define this condition and to classify the symptoms, mentions as the characteristic features the 'weakening of those emotional activities which permanently form the mainsprings of volition so that the essence of the personality becomes destroyed. There is loss of the inner unity of the activities of intellect, emotion, and volition in themselves and among one another.' In most cases there is a gradual intellectual deterioration terminating in dementia, although prolonged remissions and apparent recovery may occur.

§ 2. Etiology.

Hereditary factors play an important part in this disorder. According to Mott, successive generations of degenerate stock tend to break down at an earlier age (antedating). Thus, when one or other parent first shows signs of mental disorder in middle life, the offspring tend to break down at puberty. From his pathological researches Mott concludes that cases of dementia præcox suffer from an inborn lack of vitality which renders them unfit to weather the storms of life, to undergo the necessary adjustments of puberty, or to withstand the strains of pregnancy. A good deal of attention has been paid to what is called the 'dementia præcox personality'—that is, to the mental characteristics of the patient before the definite onset of the psychosis.

As Hoch put it: 'Like the poet, the dementia præcox is born, not made.' According to C. M. Campbell, the psychosis is the culmination of a 'long-continued period of unhealthy biological adjustments' in individuals with a constitutional inferiority. Jelliffe applies the term 'predementia præcox' to the type of personality which he regards as especially liable to develop the psychosis. Meyer regards the disorder as the consequence largely of the persistent misapplication of instincts and the maintenance of faulty habits of adjustment. Many cases appear to have been of shy seclusive habits, reserved and oversensitive to the opinions of their fellows, although often above the average in intellectual attainments. Such persons correspond to the introverts of Jung. On the other hand, the psychosis may develop on the top of definite congenital defect in persons who have always been below the average in intellectual capacity, and who may also have displayed such propensities as extreme waywardness, obstinacy, and lack of amenability. The ordinary stresses and strains of life act as precipitating factors. The psychosis commonly appears to develop after a bereavement, love affair, shock, or in connection with childbearing.

Freud has advanced the view that the disorder is due to a fixation at the auto-erotic stage of development, at which the individual is completely self-sufficing and withdraws himself from the outer reality into a world of his own fantastic creation. Jung stresses a primary psychic factor in the following words: 'Instead of assuming that some hereditary disposition or a toxæmia gives rise directly or indirectly to organic processes of disease, I incline to the view that upon the basis of predisposition, whose nature is at present unknown to us, there arises a non-adaptable psychological function which can proceed to develop into manifest mental disease; this may secondarily determine organic degeneration with its own train of symptoms.' According to this view, the psychosis develops on the following lines: Sooner or later a subject with this type of constitutional inferiority meets with some obstacle which he finds himself unable to overcome. The difficulty is met by the setting up of a complicated psychological mechanism through which the unpleasant situation becomes ignored and fantasy holds sway over fact. The clinical manifestations of dementia præcox, together with such organic changes as have been demonstrated, are, according to this view, sequels of such behaviour. The condition is sometimes termed *schizophrenia*, which means a splitting or disintegration of mind.

§ 3. Physical Signs.

Loss of weight and generally impaired health are common at the onset. A few of the cases, especially those with congenital intellectual defect, display one or more stigmata of degeneration. Stoddart lays considerable stress on the 'ape-hand,' with its lax ligaments, long tapering fingers, and thumb looking forwards instead of across the palm, all of which he considers as atavistic signs. As a rule, the patients are fairly well-developed. The blood-pressure is below the normal in many cases, especially those of the hebephrenic and katatonic variety, in whom there is possibly some failure of the adrenal function. Many katatonics have a remarkable cyanosis and œdema of the extremities, which doubtless, in most cases, is static in origin and due to prolonged immobility. The condition may be related to the vasomotor neuroses and depend upon an inbalance between the vagal and sympathetic systems. Attitudes and uniform rigidity are exhibited in katatonia, and the lips may be contracted in the form of a pig's snout. Grimaces, antics, and mannerisms are other common features. Epileptiform convulsions may occur, and attacks of rigidity such as occur in hysteria are not uncommon. The reflexes are exaggerated and the pupils react briskly and are usually dilated. There are no definite changes in the cytology and composition of the blood. The metabolism of sulphur and phosphorus have been found to be abnormal and the basal metabolic rate is lowered. After passing through the acute stage, during which the patient may be quite emaciated, the bodily condition usually improves. In fact, unless tuberculosis supervenes, the patients become fat and somewhat gross. But the actual cause of death is most often pulmonary tuberculosis.

§ 4. Pathology.

In advanced long-standing cases the brain is wasted and shows the appearances found in dementia. Alzheimer has demonstrated a gliosis of the deeper layers of the cortex. The nerve-cells undergo profound disintegration with chromatolysis, accumulation of lipoid and pigment granules, nuclear changes, and neuronophagy

Mott has discovered important changes in the ductless glands which may be summarised as follows:

1. *Testes.*—Various stages of degeneration are present, from slight abnormality in the staining reaction of the heads of the spermatozoa to marked regressive atrophy of the tubules, with great diminution or complete absence of spermatogenesis. On the whole, the more profound changes occur in cases of the longest standing. Together with these regressive changes in the tubules there is also great diminution in the number of the interstitial cells of Leydig, and degenerative changes in such as are present. Controls from other forms of insanity and from people dying of pulmonary tuberculosis (which is a common cause of death in dementia præcox) show that these

appearances are peculiar to dementia præcox and to some forms of imbecility.

2. *Ovaries* are usually much smaller than normal. On naked eye section there is a striking scarcity of maturing follicles. On microscopic examination, it is noticed that the zone of primordial follicles which forms a continuous band in normal ovaries of young adults is, in cases of dementia præcox, reduced to a few follicles, most of which show degenerative changes, affecting especially the lipoid content and the chromatin network of the nucleus and the thecal cells. The absence of follicles is compensated for by the formation of a dense fibrous stroma. Here, again, controls show that these changes appear only in dementia præcox and in certain imbeciles.

3. The thyroid and the pituitary are fairly normal, except for some fibrotic changes and diminution of cytoplasm. In the adrenals there is deficiency of lipoid in the cortex, especially in the zona fasciculata, and also degeneration of the medulla.

Various other pathological conditions have been described in dementia præcox, amongst which may be mentioned the presence of anti-ferments to the various ductless glands, determined by the Abderhalden reaction, and a congenital hypoplasia of the circulatory system.

§ 5. Mental Symptoms.

In the acute stage cognition is little affected, perception, orientation, and memory showing little abnormality. Some cases, however, are markedly confused at the outset, and the underlying condition becomes apparent only as the confusion is passing off. Most of the patients are hallucinated, and delusions also are commonly present. But the keynote of the condition is a general loss of emotional reaction, characterised by loss of natural affection, indifference to the future, and lack of interest in the present. In contrast to the general emotional apathy are the outbursts of apparently meaningless laughter and the impulsive behaviour commonly exhibited by these patients. Insight is usually present in the early stages, but is lost as the psychosis develops. At first the patients may be sensible of the subtle change which is occurring in their attitude towards environment, and they are often anxious for assistance. But so often, in spite of every effort, the rapport between physician and patient gradually weakens, and the patient retires into himself as the deteriorating process goes on.

The disease has been classified into four varieties:

Simple.—This consists of a progressive mental deterioration occurring about the time of puberty or early adult life, commonly in individuals who already display some congenital intellectual defect. There is gross emotional dullness. Hallucinations and delusions are not a prominent feature of this variety, and may be absent. Mannerisms and negativism may be present. There is rapid progress to dementia to the extent that the patient becomes unable to attend to his personal needs.

Hebephrenia (*hebe*=youth) is more common in males and in the third decade. Frequently at onset the patient complains of headache and malaise, and appears to be in indifferent health. He then becomes depressed, dull, and apathetic, tends to avoid the company of others, and may be irritable at any interference. Partial insight may be retained for some time and the patient may realise that some change has come over him, although he tends to ascribe it to some external influence. Suicidal attempts are not uncommon. Later he becomes childish and inconsequent in behaviour, and his depression may be broken by outbursts of giggling and laughing, thus offering a marked contrast to the consistent depression of melancholia with which this disorder may be confused. In many cases there are fantastic delusions, also hallucinations, especially of hearing. Mannerisms, antics, and other peculiarities of behaviour are also to be observed. All these symptoms become less prominent as dementia supervenes.

Katatonia.—This is rather more common in females and occurs generally before the age of twenty-five. Three forms are recognised:

1. *Depression.*—After a prodromal period of indefinite ill-health there develop insomnia, depression, limitation of activity, and a gradual withdrawal from contact with environment. The patients often give expression to delusions of a persecutory or self-accusatory nature, and hallucinations are commonly present. A peculiar rigidity develops in these patients which is uniform in distribution, thus differing from that of melancholia with its distinctive attitude. Moreover, these patients have not the characteristic facial expression of the melancholic, but grimace and display curious tremors and spasms of the facial muscles, especially a pursing or protrusion of the lips. Negativism is often present in the form of resistance to any attention, mutism, and refusal of food. Sometimes a phrase may be repeated over and over (*verbigeration*). Some of these cases appear to make a complete recovery, but most become demented.

2. *Stupor.*—This occurs most commonly as a sequel to katatonic depression. The patient sits or stands in various attitudes, is mute, or verbigerates a little, or repeats what is said to him (*echolalia*). Mannerisms are very common. The receptive side of mentation is little affected, perception is good, and if he recovers the patient may be able to give a good account of the acute stage of his illness and of the events which were happening around him. On testing his sensation with a pin, he may display no sign except a slight reddening of the face, and there is no attempt to avoid the painful stimulus. Vasomotor disturbances such as peripheral cyanosis and œdema are common in this variety. *Echopraxia,* the imitation of the actions

of others, and *Flexibilitas cerea*, the holding of the limbs in any attitude in which they are placed by the observer, are other common signs.

3. *Excitement.*—This may occur *de novo* or may be incidental to other forms of dementia præcox. It may easily be mistaken for acute mania, but the points of difference are as follows:

Acute Mania.	**Katatonic Excitement.**
Behaviour. — Press of activity, mostly purposive.	Absurd, stereotyped, purposeless, often violent and impulsive.
Speech. — Flight of ideas.	Confused and incoherent; often a hotch-potch, or ' word-salad.'
Negativism.—Absent.	Present.
Emotional Tone.—Exalted.	Deficient or absent.
Hallucinations. — Absent or insignificant.	Present.
Sensation. — Hyperæsthetic.	Anæsthetic.

Behaviour may be degraded in the extreme, and the patients may be most difficult to manage owing to their resistiveness.

Dementia Paranoides.—Delusions and hallucinations are very prominent in this form. Minor degrees of depression or excitement are not infrequent in the early stages. Other signs, such as mannerisms, inconsequent behaviour, and impulsive outbursts with general emotional dullness, are present. The delusions may be either grandiose or persecutory. They tend to be fantastic, extravagant, and constantly changing in character, and do not appear to fit into any logical system, thus contrasting with other delusional states. The patients commonly complain that their thoughts are read or that their brains are controlled. The hallucinations may affect all senses, and, like the delusions, are bizarre and mysterious.

'Electrical' feelings are common and are ascribed to some outside influence. Dementia develops within a few years, and the delusions and hallucinations become less prominent.

§ 6. Classification.

Kraepelin classified the different forms of dementia præcox as follows:

1. According to course:
   (*a*) Insidiously progressive.
   (*b*) Cases with remissions.
   (*c*) Arrested cases, with varying degrees of deterioration.
   (*d*) Cases making an apparently complete recovery.

2. According to the clinical picture:
   (*a*) Simple dementia.
   (*b*) Depressed forms.
   (*c*) Stuporose forms.
   (*d*) Excited forms.
   (*e*) Confused and agitated forms.
   (*f*) Hebephrenia.
   (*g*) Paranoid dementia.

It is important to note that cases may retain the same group of signs and symptoms throughout the course of the disease or the same patient may pass through different varieties of dementia præcox, and mixed forms occur which cannot be placed definitely under any one of the above headings. Cases seen in mental hospitals are necessarily fairly well defined. In fact, a large proportion of the chronic cases in asylums are schizophrenics. The growth of out-patient clinics is leading to the recognition of the fact that there are many cases of a milder type, either arrested or running an extremely slow course, who probably never reach the certifiable stage, and who can carry on with only moderately impaired efficiency.

§ 7. Diagnosis.

In most cases this disorder has a gradual slow onset. Due attention should be paid to the history of the personality before the development of definite mental symptoms, especially of any change of disposition occurring about puberty. The 'shut-in,' reticent, seclusive, non-adaptable types of person appear to be especially liable to develop this psychosis. Dementia præcox may resemble the following conditions:

(*a*) *Imbecility* and other forms of congenital defect. This depends upon the history of the patient, although the possibility of superadded 'præcox' symptoms must not be overlooked.

(*b*) *Confusional States.*—There is frequently a history of antecedent physical or mental stress. The patients are grossly disorientated, amnesic, imperceptive, and analgesic, yet display a considerable degree of emotion. There is a katatonic form of acute confusion in which the patient is mute and stuporose and inaccessible to mental examination. Such cases can only be diagnosed in the course of the illness. In the more severe forms of katatonic excitement or depression there may be a large confusional element from exhaustion.

(*c*) *Manic-Depressive Insanity.*—Katatonic excitement and depression simulate mania and melancholia respectively. The history is of importance with regard to the existence of the præcox personality or of previous attacks of mania or melancholia. Such accompaniments of dementia præcox as impulsive outbursts, verbigeration, stereotypy, and foolish inconsequent behaviour should give a clue as to the real nature of the excitement or depression.

(*d*) *Stupor* occurs in such a variety of conditions that it will be considered more fully later.

(*e*) *Delusional States, especially Paranoia.*—The latter occurs at a later period of life, usually in the fourth decade, and continues for many years without disintegration of the personality. Disordered judgment is the outstanding feature. The delusions are fixed and fit into a definite system, though increasing in complexity. Alcoholic states and general paralysis must be excluded. Paraphrenia, another delusional state, is considered in the next chapter.

(*f*) *Neurasthenia.*—Fatigue symptoms are complained of, such as inability to concentrate, tired feelings, and sense of pressure on the head. But there is complete insight and a real anxiety to get well. In dementia præcox, on the other hand, there is, sooner or later, indifference with a tendency to ascribe the condition to some external agency such as hypnotic action.

§ 8. Treatment.

Rest in bed is desirable for most cases in the acute stage, with a liberal diet. Tube feeding may be necessary when the patient refuses to take an adequate diet. Toxic foci should be dealt with, but with discrimination and restraint. The administration of testicular or ovarian extracts has not been followed by any marked success, but intensive thyroid therapy sometimes stirs these patients out of their lethargy. Extract of thyroid should be given in increasing doses until a physiological effect is produced and maintained for a week or more, when the dosage may gradually be reduced. But it cannot be said that thyroid deficiency is common in dementia præcox. In view of the frequency of low blood pressure, however, especially in the katatonic variety, the injection of 5 minims or more of 1 in 1,000 adrenalin solution several times daily has been advocated and is sometimes followed by improvement.

The Insulin treatment introduced by Sakel in 1935 and Cardiazol Convulsion Therapy applied by von

Meduna in 1934 are both productive of considerable improvement, if not complete remission in about 70 per cent. of cases of schizophrenia of recent development. The insulin treatment is usually more pleasant for the patient, but is harder to carry out and is attended by greater liability to dangerous complications. An average course of treatment consists of from twenty to thirty or more coma hours. The Cardiazol Convulsion Therapy should be given twice or thrice a week until a satisfactory degree of improvement has taken place, up to a maximum of twenty-five convulsions during a course. It is important to keep the patients as fully occupied as possible on the days in between the treatments. Occupational therapy, as far as possible selected to suit the needs and abilities of each case, plays an important part in the care of those who have to remain in an institution. A fair proportion of cases who fail to recover after passing through the acute stage settle down to institutional life and carry on an automatic type of existence, doing useful routine work under supervision.

Although recent methods of treatment are proving so much more effective than psychotherapy alone, the possibility of prophylaxis must not be overlooked. The study of abnormality in children, of faulty methods of upbringing, and of the various causes productive of mental ill-health, will all help in the detection of the non-adaptable type of individual who is liable to develop a psychosis. It may be possible in such a case so to rearrange the environment as to remove him from contact with such factors as might cause a definite breakdown, and yet to retain his usefulness as a social unit. Much may be done by placing psychopaths in suitable employment, so that they may avoid severe competition. The general practitioner who comes into contact with cases in their early stages forms the first and the most important link in the chain of measures designed to deal with the early treatment of mental disorders. If he has not the time or the inclination for handling these cases as modern psychiatry indicates, he should at least refer them to the psychiatrist, rather than dismiss them with a 'placebo' or neglect the serious developments which are likely to occur in any mental patient who is treated without proper understanding.

Lightning Source UK Ltd.
Milton Keynes UK
UKOW050632300312

189888UK00001B/32/P

9 781447 431206